# RIVER
# OF
# USED TO BE

## Reflections of an Ozarks Editor

# RIVER OF USED TO BE

## Reflections of an Ozarks Editor

## Jim Hamilton

Seven Oaks Publishing Company
Conway, Arkansas

Copyright 1994 by James E. Hamilton.
All rights reserved. This book, or parts thereof,
may not be reproduced in any form without permission.
Published by Seven Oaks Publishing Company
P.O. Box 1103, Conway, Arkansas 72033

Printed in the United States of America

10 9 8 7 6 5 4 3 2 1

Library of Congress Catalog Card Number: 93-086563

ISBN 0-9630829-3-0

First Edition, 1994

Executive Director and Project Editor: W.C. Jameson
Associate Editor: LaTonya Pate
Cover Photography: Steve Schibler

**SEVEN OAKS PUBLISHING COMPANY
CONWAY, ARKANSAS**

**In Memory Of**

ANGELA JO HAMILTON

December 31, 1971 - April 21, 1991

# Contents

Forward by Suzann Ledbetter / xi

Introduction / 1

**Part One: More Than A Place To Live / 3**

    A Good Place To Live / 5
    No Place Like This Place / 8
    Old-Timers / 9
    Lumberjack Days / 12
    Catchin' Crawdads / 14
    Greasy Creek / 16
    Glory / 18
    Bawl of the Hound / 21
    Keeping Cool / 23
    Milking Cows / 25
    Owls / 29
    Last of the Good Old Days / 31
    River of Used To Be / 33

**Part Two: Grandma's Roses / 35**

    Grandma's Roses / 37
    Grandma Never Watched TV / 38
    Mother's Days / 41
    Dad's Day / 42
    A House Too Quiet / 44
    A Hole In The House / 45
    Magnetic Tapestry / 47
    House That Was A Home / 48

**Part Three: God Owns The Woods /51**

My Woods / 53
Fourth of July at Long Lane / 53
Rivers / 55
Hometown / 56
Gentle Spirits Of Union Mound / 57
Thistles / 59
Buttered Toast / 61
Welcome Return To Ozarks / 62
Windyville Happy Homemakers / 64
Comments on Chewin' / 66
Discourse On Pleasures Of Fishing / 68
Tailgates / 73
Sidewalks and Porches / 75
He Knew Cars / 77
Accident Victim / 79

**Part Four: Winterfall To Frost / 81**

Winterfall / 83
Winter Courting / 84
Every Snow Should So Softly Fall / 85
Camp of the Frozen Coffee Pot / 86
Signs of Spring / 92
Battle For The Bean Patch / 94
Tales Told In The Face Of An Axe / 95
Life's The Berries / 98
Dandelions / 100
Images Of Summer / 101
Hot And Dry / 102
Cool Water / 103
Tugs Of Instinct / 105
First Frost / 106
Splashy October / 107
Winter Blows Petals From Marigolds / 108

**Part Five: Tinseltime** / 111

Tinseltime / 113
Cedar Tree Tradition / 115
Picture Of Despair / 119
A Christmas Gift / 120
Holiday Season Like Vacation / 123
The Truth About Santa / 124
Santa Drops In On Cinder Creek / 126
Elmo, The Stable Elf / 131
Celebration Of Christmas Promise / 135

**Part Six: Hambone Ridge** / 137

A Place To Slip Away / 139
Halloween / 139
Cloyd And Brody On Anvil Point /141
Bucket Seat / 144
Last Day Of Coffeepot Rock / 145

Acknowledgements / end page

# Forward
## by
## Suzann Ledbetter

Whenever the spirit moves me to sit a spell with a cup of coffee and a good book, Jim Hamilton's **River Of Used To Be** will be waiting on the shelf to lend another enjoyable interlude. That's the kind of book it is: One that can't be put down while you're reading it, and one you'll reach for again and again.

Using words elegant in their simplicity, Jim paints memorable and immediately identifiable images in the reader's mind that are as true to life's vagaries as those the late Norman Rockwell depicted on canvas.

His powerful prose captures the essence of the Ozarks region, her people, and her spirit. Although I am, like Jim, a native Ozarker, I had long ago turned blind eyes and deaf ears to the living legacy surrounding me. **River Of Used To Be** not only reintroduced me to my birthright, it will introduce all who read it to the Ozarks' priceless treasures: Its hardscrabble hills, wildflowered valleys, fishin' holes, and the tough, tender-hearted folks who proudly call it home.

Jim's childhood memory of playing "store" in his Grandma Daly's kitchen; the bittersweetness of his high school graduation and immediate draft eligibility; battles fought with groundhogs for the year's homegrown tomato harvest; the heart-heaviness that comes from being a small town newspaperman and knowing, odds are, every siren heard is wailing for a friend, neighbor, or God forbid, a family member, reveal their creator's character and word craftsmanship.

There is wisdom contained within these pages, and humor, and heart. But Jim doesn't relate these truisms in that smack-you-upside-the-head style other columnists are famous for. Like a delicate whiff of woodsmoke on a cool, autumn night, Jim's philosophies of life as he knows it drift by easy, but linger long.

I'm grateful to Jim for allowing me to share his recollections and musings, his love of the Ozarks and her people, his poignancy for times past and almost forgotten, for making me laugh, and for making me think.

I hope someday you'll have a chance to swap howdys with Jim Hamilton and maybe trade a few tales with him over a cup of coffee. But if not, when you finish **River Of Used To Be**, you'll think of the man who wrote it as a new-found friend.

*Suzann Ledbetter is the author of* **The Toast Always Lands Jelly-Side Down** *and is a contributing editor to Family Circle magazine.*

# Introduction

I was born into the Missouri Ozarks on December 30, 1947. That incident of birth, however, did not, of itself, make me a child of the Ozarks.

The protective nuzzling of a bluetick hound named Frosty; warm summer evenings catfishing down at Potter's Ford on the Pomme de Terre River; Jersey cows that gave rich, yellow milk; the sweet smell of lespedeza hay thrown from the barnloft in winter; the serenade of whippoorwills; and the heavy, calloused hands of old-timers who shared the sagacity of their seasons--it is these and ten thousand more experiences which have made me an Ozarker. And it is these experiences of growing up and living in the Ozarks which are reflected in this book.

Folks in large sections of Missouri and Arkansas, as well as parts of eastern Olklahoma, lay claim to a share of the Ozarks. Geographers have no touble defining its bounds, but for the rest of us it's a little tougher. The true Ozarks are not so much a place on the map as they are a place in the heart of the people who call these mountains, glades, bottoms, and prairies home.

Neither birth nor habitation alone make an Ozarker. That unique state of mind requires no less than a union of the heart and spirit with the Ozarks and her people. For it is their unique, unpretentious character and culture which sets the Ozarks apart from similar geography. No mountains equal those of the Ozarks when seen through the hearts, hands, and souls of the

## Jim Hamilton

people who draw life from them.

*River of Used To Be* was not written as a book about the Ozarks. It is simply a collection of newspaper columns written by an Ozarker. The subjects are diverse, ranging from nostalgia to pure fiction, and only occasionally make direct reference to the Ozarks.

The selections were originally published in the *Buffalo Reflex*, a 124 year-old weekly newspaper in Dallas County, Missouri, which I've had the privilige to edit since 1978. As an Ozarks newspaperman, I've shared the joy and heartbreak of folks in a place where "community" still means people, not just a name on a map. The columns in *River of Used To Be* were written for and about the people of my Ozarks community.

The Ozarks are different things to different people. For me it's the timbered ridges, the kindred souls, the rocky earth of my tangled roots, and the twilight reflections on a meandering *River of Used To Be*.

Jim Hamilton
June, 1993

# Part One

# MORE THAN A PLACE TO LIVE

### Growing Up And Living In The Ozarks

## A Good Place to Live

All things considered, Buffalo, Missouri, is a pretty good place to live.

Folks may complain about some things--I guess I do my share--but, in an imperfect world, Buffalo has about as few imperfections as anyplace. One of the best things about Buffalo, or one of the worst, depending on your point of view, is that it is a small country town.

As a small country town, it has a lot of little characteristics that seperate it from all other towns. These things may be good, or they may be bad, but mostly, they're just like noses--some may be big, some may be small, some may be pretty, and some may be ugly, but who's to say which is better. That kind of depends on the rest of the face and what you're looking for in faces.

In any case, I've given some thought to some of the character traits of Buffalo and have come up with a few things to help the rest of the world recongnize the town when they pass through, come to visit, or move in to stay.

You know you are in Buffalo when:

* You can buy a loaf of bread from the Chief of Police at his wife's store on evenings, noon hours, and weekends.

* The Municipal Judge is not only a sweet, silver-haired, little old lady, but a great-grandmother as well.

# Jim Hamilton

* City Council meeting dates are moved because the scheduled day coincides with the mayor's bowling night.
* The County Fair Board reschedules its meeting night because the City Council's change conflicts with its meeting night.
* You can't climb the social ladder without a four-wheel-drive pick-up.
* You can't find a good or bad side of town. The affluent and the impoverished are quite comfortable living next door to one another.
* The most exciting thing for kids to do on a Saturday night is drive around the square. . . and around, and around, and. . . .
* It snows and the city attorney's secretary shovels the sidewalk.
* Most public offices in the courthouse close for an hour at midday.
* More news is broadcast at the barbershop than on the local radio station.
* The hottest news in town is old hat in the favorite coffee shop before the favorite newspaper gets wind of it.
* Your landlord knows you've bought a new house before you do.
* It seems like the only folks in town who aren't related by blood or marriage are you and me.
* You have three addresses: a route and box number for the Post Office, a street number for the city meter reader, and a more reliable "three houses down from the old so-and-so house" for everyone else.
* You are better off not to let anyone know you have a college education, a savings account, or a tie.

# River Of Used To Be

\* You discover it seems that the only real "natives" were born here before World War II.

\* A discussion between the local veterinarian, a truck driver, a farmer or two, and an insurance agent is a school board meeting.

\* Folks in town may never change the world, but the rest of the world is even less likely to change them.

\* You find that two things can stop spring haying: rain and summer league softball.

\* You notice that light poles at one end of the rodeo arena at the fairgrounds are lower than at the other end, and the other poles stairstep to the highest point, in direct proportion to FAA airspace requirements because the airport is next door.

\* You see the Superintendent of Schools coaching third grade girls basketball.

\* You realize you could spend all afternoon looking and never find the oak grove in "Oak Grove Addition."

\* You discover senior citizens club members outnumber the Girl Scouts, Campfire Girls, and Boy Scouts all combined.

\* You discover the only things you really need to get along in town are a good sense of humor, a ready smile, a crumpled pouch of "Red Man", a pair of cowboy boots with manure caked in the instep, a hound dog, and time for a cup of coffee.

# Jim Hamilton

## No Place Like This Place

There's no place in the world quite like Dallas County.

Take that any way you want. I take it as good.

We're a lot like most other rural communities. We wave at one another on the road, say "howdy" when we meet on the sidewalk, and stop to visit in the grocery store.

Some places it's just not safe to exchange friendly greetings. City folks think you're strange. Maybe even funny. Down here it's downright rude to walk past somebody without saying a word, or at least giving a nod. Folks think you're uppity, mad at 'em, or from out of town.

Living here forces you to be friendly, but folks here are more than just friendly; they're quick to become friends.

It can get on your nerves. Everybody knows your business. But, you'll never have to go through anything alone, good times or bad. Folks here are real neighbors.

It's no revelation that Dallas County is different from the rest of the world. Anyone who stops here long enough for a cup of coffee will soon figure that out.

What's not so quickly evident is just how much different we are from most of the counties all around us.

It seems folks in other towns are bent on getting ahead there. We're mostly content with just getting by.

It's not that folks here aren't ambitious, or that they don't want to make a lot of money, live in big houses, or drive a Mercedes. But, there's not many folks I know who are driven to make a big splash just to impress or outdo their neighbors.

# River Of Used To Be

This is about the least pretentious place you'll find. Ostentatious displays of wealth and affluence don't impress many of us. Lots of folks here could drive Mercedes's or live in mansions, but they don't. Maybe that's why they can.

Appearances don't tell much about a person's wealth here. Princes and paupers drink from the same coffee pot, say "howdy" to one another on the street, and leave outsiders wondering which is the richer.

Not many places in the world like that.

No place in the world like this.

## Old-Timers

I recall when old-timers were salty rascals who might remember when the fastest thing on the road was a bay gelding of uncertain ancestry which somebody's Uncle Jack won in a poker game.

These days, it seems, an old-timer is anyone who can remember when cars had six-volt batteries and vacuum windshield wipers (they stopped dead when you put the pedal down on a hill).

Soon enough, anyone who can remember carburetors will be an old-timer, too.

The world is changing so fast that old-timers aren't so old as they used to be. I look around, just a graying baby-boomer, and start to feel a bit of an old-timer myself.

Day-by-day, I'm finding more in common with the experiences of my dad and granddad. Too much that I recall may never be seen by babies born today. I feel like a real old-timer when I remember:

# Jim Hamilton

* Fishing in Greasy Creek near Elkland, catching bullheads, bass, and big black perch from deep, spring-fed pools. The same stream is now a dry branch most of the year.
* Giant bass in the Pomme de Terre River near Fair Grove. Before the lake was built they came up in the spring--bass in the eight to nine-pound range. The river teemed with fish year-round. There was no better place.
* Fishing for suckers below the old steel bridge over the Niangua River near Charity. We walked out to a little island and caught towsacks-full on worms.
* The old train depot in Springfield, Missouri, and the nickel Coke machine in the back.
* Commercial Street in Springfield when folks could walk without fear day and night, and buy anything they needed there, go to the bank, the doctor, and the drug store.
* When buses interchanged on the Springfield city square. Nobody had heard of "Park Central" or "Battlefield Mall".
* Cars rumbling over the bricks in Kings Avenue at Southwest Missouri State College.
* Route 66 running through Springfield.
* Dickerson Park Zoo with monkeys in the old Swinea Building and lions and bears in stone cages.
* Lanky Planky on Campbell Street Lumber Company trucks.
* Yellow Bonnet Foods. The Exchange and grocery store doing business in Elkland. The Exchange on the square in Buffalo.
* Silver Dollar City before music shows, crafts festivals and rides in rubber rafts. My first time there

# River Of Used To Be

our bus parked on the square. Marvel Cave was the main attraction. Some folks had been living down there in the name of science. Water ran uphill in the old miner's cabin.

* Branson at the bottom of the hill, nestled in a bend of Lake Taneycomo. Table Rock was new. There was a "77-Sunset Strip" on TV, but no '76 Strip for Ozarks tourists.

* The sharp bend in Highway 32 south of the square in Buffalo.

Times have changed. Remembering just how much in a few short years makes many of us feel like "old-timers". I wonder what the old-timers of twenty years down the road will fondly remember:

* Gas for just $1 a gallon?
* New cars for just $20,000?
* Wild turkey? Deer? Fishing in the Niangua?
* Landfills and $6 a month trash rates?
* Woodburning stoves?
* Drinking water straight from the well?
* Family farms and milk cows?
* Weekly newspapers?
* This ol' newspaper editor?

Whatever their memories, it's a sure bet that in two decades those kids glued in front of MTV today will have witnessed accelerated changes. The world of 2011 will just vaguely resemble ours. Too many woods and free-running streams, I fear, will have been lost to memories, and the old-timers of that age will barely be turning gray.

# Jim Hamilton

## Lumberjack Days

I was eight years old the first time I remember picking up an axe.

It was a new single-bit axe. I took it out to the orchard and commenced to hacking on a log. The handle had an odd twist to it, the head seemed off-balance, and it wouldn't cut butter. Just as well--we didn't need any wood cut, let alone any butter.

The winter I turned ten we had moved to a brushy thirty-nine acres in Dallas County, Missouri, and the handle of a double-bitted axe began to feel comfortable in my hands. We had sprouts to chop and wood to cut. In the season that followed, I learned to swing an axe like Mickey Mantle swung his bat.

Before I'd reached full size, I could lay into a tree and make saucer-sized wood chips fly. I split firewood and fence posts with a sharp axe, a steady swing, and a good eye.

From the time I was nine going on ten, we burned wood at home and cut acres of sprouts, as well as kept my grandma's old wood cookstove well-supplied.

Not only an axe, but splitting wedges and an old twenty-pound railroad hammer became my friends, along with a heavy-bladed bucksaw and a limber crosscut. I was nearly grown before dad introduced me to a cantankerous old chainsaw.

Sure, like other kids, I played Cowboys and Indians, and imagined I was Davy Crockett and Daniel Boone.

But, is it any surprise that the legendary woodsman who intrigued me most was a burly giant who could fairly swing an axe? Paul Bunyan, of course.

## River Of Used To Be

Boone.

But, is it any surprise that the legendary woodsman who intrigued me most was a burly giant who could fairly swing an axe? Paul Bunyan, of course.

I fiddled with sprouts and scrubby trees, while Paul with his blue ox, Babe, cleared entire states of their trees.

Along the way of growing up, I seemed fitted best in flannel shirts and stocking caps, work boots and leather gloves. It was years later when first appeared my Bunyanesque beard. But, early on, the die was cast. One brother became Izzak Walton, another Pecos Bill, and another the Gray Ghost of the Confederacy (John Singleton Mosby), while I became a lumberjack.

So, don't think me too odd when you see me out in a flannel shirt and stocking cap, looking little like a newspaper man, and more like a storybook lumberjack. I'm just being what something inexplicably ticking inside says I am: A boy raised with an axe in his hand.

I now swing a chainsaw more than an axe, though I keep one handy and sharpened to shave whiskers from blackjack trunks. I love the smell of sawdust, the warmth of a fire built in the woods, the feel of bark on my hands, and the thwack of an axe falling through a straight-grained chunk of wood.

Like an old Yankee loves his Louisville Slugger, I love the feel of an axe, swung round from the shoulders to the base of a tree. It feels like a homer when the big chips fly. There are no fans to cheer when it goes over the fence, but somewhere, just over my shoulder, the giant Bunyan watches, and smiles.

### Jim Hamilton

## Catchin' Crawdads

There was a time when catchin' crawdads was about as much fun as a 10-year-old kid and his little brother could have. It was wet, on-your-hands-and-knees-in-the mud warm weather fun, nobody telling us to keep clean, and nobody wondering what we were doing in a mudhole beside the road.

We were catchin' crawdads, or "crawdeads", as we called 'em, for fishbait. No fish could resist the soft brown crawdads we gathered, the largest no longer than our little fingers.

Our crawdad hole was really no creek, just a hole the size of a bathtub at the end of a pipe under the road. Water stood in it most of the year, as it did in pockets all along the wet-weather branch that crossed the place.

Today, there's a pond just across the road and a house up the hill. Back then, though, the branch was fed by a ditch through a wooded hollow. Across the road was a big woods. The road was gravel, with not much traffic. Since then, our road has become civilized. The woods have been cut, the gravel paved, and the crawdad hole is just a memory.

But, I remember when I was ten.

Sometimes we would catch the crawdads with our hands, their pinchers too small to hurt us much. But, the most effective method was to dip through the muddied pothole with half an old minnow trap. In just minutes we'd have a minnow bucket crawling with craws. The next part was the most fun of all; we'd go fishing.

I've seined a lot of crawdads since then, but none were better bait than those brown craws from the road

## River Of Used To Be

ditch.

Anybody with any river sense knows there's a lot of difference in crawdads. Soft-shelled ones make the best bait, and brown ones seem to do better than the green ones. Some creeks yield up brown ones, usually from slower water. Fast water, like in the Niangua River, has lots of hard green ones. They work good in that river; the goggle-eye and smallmouth are used to 'em.

Crawdads of any color go by various names. Some folks call 'em "crawfish". School teachers think they're "crayfish"; I always called 'em "crawdeads", and that didn't suit my teachers. I recall an argument I had with a teacher when she counted "crawdead" wrong on a science paper. She insisted the correct answer was "crayfish", and I insisted she was a supercilious idiot. I'm sure neither one of us has changed our opinion.

Crawdads grown past the bait stage have in recent years found a place on fancy restaurant menus.

Over the years I've caught plenty of crawdads big enough to eat, but I used the tails for bait, rather than for some Cajun creation. I just hated to drop a notch on the food chain.

Catfishing at McDaniel Lake, on the Sac River north of Springfield, used to produce some sizeable craws, crusty centenarians which were all head and pinchers.

I recall similar luck one night catfishing with liver on the Niangua. But, rather than throw the craws in the creek, I was just mad because they weren't channel cat, and tossed 'em back.

All my life I've put up with crawdads as a baitfishing nuisance, and never exacted the ultimate revenge. I've never eaten 'em.

# Jim Hamilton

The only crawdads I've eaten were too high-falutin' to be caught stealing fishbait. They were cultured "crawfish" fried up and served on a bed of rice. Probably thought themselves little lobsters, rather than common crawdads.

But, don't be fooled by gourmet names; these epicurean aristocrats have cousins building mud chimneys in swampy fields, hiding under rocks in Greasy Creek, and towing fish heads in holes at Bennett Spring.

They may even have some family in a crawdad hole where kids play still, along some country road.

## Greasy Creek

I grew up drinking water from Greasy Creek.

I wouldn't advise it today. The days when we filled old milk cans with drinking water have become history, just as have the waterholes where we filled them.

Those were the days when Greasy was a creek, and not a sullen summertime sewer of algae and slime, those distant days when its upper reaches bubbled with springs and ran clear and cold across gravel-bottom pools glittering with shiner minnows.

Greasy Creek started along a hollow just east of the Dallas County bootheel, just a ditch under the road near Elkland. Fed by springs and smaller streams, it grew steadily larger before crossing into Dallas County, and winding its way toward Buffalo, Missouri, finally joining the Niangua River northeast of town.

It looks the same today on county maps; but, it isn't.

Across the road and through the woods, Greasy

## River Of Used To Be

Creek was about a half-mile from the house. As youngsters, my Brother Russell and I would often walk there to catch stringers of perch, little bass, and bullheads. We never counted on finding lots of big fish in the creek across the road, but we always counted on finding water. There were some stretches where the stream slowed to a trickle across the rocky shallows. Under tree roots were deep holes, and in many places, cold spring-fed holes where watercress carpeted the surface in green. We never hesitated to munch on a spicy mouthful. The only pollution that concerned us was waterbugs.

A couple miles from the house, a country road crossed the creek. Today, that crossing is just a slab of concrete and the creek is mostly a wet-weather branch. Summertime the water stops running and green moss clogs the waterhole like old paint rags.

This is the old waterhole. When the pump went out and we had to haul water to the house, this is where we drew our drinking water. It was, in those days, as pure and clean as a draught from the deepest well, except for a minnow or two.

It was in this hole, too, where as kids we cooled off after a long day in the hayfields. It wasn't deep--no more than four feet at the base of the sycamore tree. But, it was cool and clean.

Down another mile or so another bridge crosses Greasy. It was there we seined minnows year-round. Steelbacks schooled tight against the limestone and gravel bottom, ducking under brush and roots where the stream turned and swirled.

Now, the water hardly runs in any season. I've not stopped in years to see if there's any reason to bring a seine.

Halfway to Buffalo, at the ford near Dogtown, Greasy was a teeming stream in earlier years. There, too, the creek withdraws in all but wet seasons. Nearer Buffalo, in the rainy season Greasy yet musters the force to push aside aging concrete slabs. But, in summer, even as it nears the Niangua, it is a lazy stream, an aging creek of clogged arteries and failing energies.

It's hard to imagine the brash, frontier stream that local legend claims overturned a trader's wagonload of bacon, and earned itself the unflattering name, Greasy Creek.

Yet, it's harder still, when crossing that little slab just past the Dallas-Webster county line, that the stagnant cesspool seething around the peeling roots of a sycamore tree was our watering hole and summertime cooling-off place.

That was the upper Greasy Creek of another time, but, sadly, of no other place.

## Glory

I saw the movie *Glory*. I remember a captain's innocent face, his chivalrous carriage, and noble calling. I recall the flag waving, drums beating, and cadence of glory. It was a movie, only make-believe.

But, the emotions were real. I recognized them from my youth when I was as fresh-faced as a Union captain before Bull Run.

We are now poised on the brink of war against Iraq, brought to the battlefront by patriotic rhetoric, illusions of chivalry, and glory--knights prepared to de-

## River Of Used To Be

fend Lady Liberty in a land she has never known. I recognize the emotions and the fantasies from my own fresh-faced youth.

I remember, too, a boy I knew in school. We were classmates for several years, but more adversaries than friends. We once put on gloves and pounded one another in junior high gym. Nobody won, but we were kind of friends after that.

His family moved and he left during high school, though he came back to visit now and then. He had to show off the new car he got for his sixteenth birthday.

After high school he joined the Marines and went to Vietnam. It was sometime in '66, as I recall, and he was the last man in his unit to fall. I don't have much reason to remember Jack; he was never a close friend, but he was the first soldier I knew to die. I'll never forget his face. It was fresh, and etched with "glory."

There was another fellow about my age near home. We went to different schools, but we both called Elkland home. We worked together some, fixing fence and shoveling corn. He was one of the hardest-working, toughest guys I knew. I started college and he joined the Navy. The last time I saw him was in uniform at our church. Sometime later I heard C.C. had gone down on a plane out of Hawaii. Just a couple years ago I learned he was still listed as MIA. I see his face, fresh as ever, and his shoulders bent to a shovelful of corn, when I drive by his folks' old place.

Glory, however, eludes this mind's eye.

I was in ROTC in college. Back in the late sixties, all freshmen and sophomore men at Southwest Missouri State College had to take it. The football practice fields served as drill fields to thousands of reluctant college

## Jim Hamilton

boy soldiers. Lording over the masses of ROTC students was a cadre of advanced ROTC cadets. They took it seriously. They didn't have to be in green--they wanted to be. In 1968, few of us wanted to graduate in Army green with one yellow bar. Truth be known, by that time most of us had heard enough about Vietnam.

    I knew enough to know I didn't want to go. "Cannon fodder" they called second lieutenants. I wonder if they were. I yet remember faces of cadet officers I didn't like at all and wonder whatever became of their fresh young faces, how many came home to bask in the "glory" that followed Vietnam.

    I was never in the war, though I got to wear a special ribbon because the U.S. was at war. I was an Air Force newspaper editor in North Carolina. That's where they sent me, and it suited me fine. North Carolina had a more homey ring than North Vietnam.

    At times I wish I'd seen Vietnam. It's one of those things folks don't like to do, but like to have done. But, I've no doubt that I wouldn't be who I am today, had Southeast Asia washed my face. Better or worse, I'll never know.

    Though I was never a real soldier, I was proud of the uniform and the stripes I wore. I didn't go far, but I would have gone anywhere my orders sent me. When you're in uniform, you don't have many choices. You don't make policy, start wars, or avoid them.

    Saddam Hussein may have provided the United States no course but one which leads to war.

    Yet, no matter how noble or valorous the cause, glory will comfort us little when the drumbeat fades and the flag-draped boxes are flown home.

    The price of freedom is paid in blood, a truth

both noble and tragic. The cost may be unavoidable, yet for each bit of freedom, we erase a fresh young face.

As a half-million Americans watch the front lines, committed to fight, remember their names and faces.

Our battle flags unfurl, the drumbeat cadence rises, nervous soliders sweat in their trenches, clutching rifles and family pictures to their breasts, the commander's sword is raised, the bugler's lips to the brass, and breathless moments pass.

On this cold January night, I am yet unsure what is wrong and what is right, though an awful fear in my stomach tells me we must, and we will fight.

Yet my rally to arms is slow, as fresh young faces of another generation in glory days linger, and I wonder if wars are ever truly won.

## Bawl of the Hound

Sittin' here trying to concentrate on writing. . . suddenly through the screen window drifts the long coarse bawl--"Arrooowww"--of a 'coon hound.

There's a cool edge on the air that slips through the screen. On it rides the recurring bawl.

Concentration's shot. Whatever serious and profound thoughts might have been about to congeal are blown away like fog before a wind.

The hound bawls again. . . maybe he's tied. I picture the hound--a bluetick secured in the back of an old Ford pickup.

Suggestions of profitable thought are replaced immediately by visions of a sixteen-year old me, lantern in hand, shuffling through the leaves, listening for the

# Jim Hamilton

hounds on a late November night.

My memory sketches the view from a hill overlooking a frosty, moonlit Jones Creek bottom. I remember the hunt too well: it was 18 years ago and we didn't strike a good track at all. Too bright, too frosty. I don't remember if my hands were cold or hot.

The bawl of the hound drifts in again, jostles my thoughts, spurs remembrance of our own hounds bawling on a distant ridge.

The bitch pup Kate taps a tree. I leave Dad to catch up with her, racing ahead, Radar Lite and our weathered Winchester .22 rifle in hand, through brush and briars, leaping leaf-filled gullies, hellbent for a treed coon in the Handley Woods, guided by the bark of Kate, a piercing long bawl that cuts across the hollers like a country yodel, and by the low, steady, raspy bark of Kate's mom, ol' Babe.

Now and then I hear the coarse deep bark of Blue.

Blue--he was the best natural pup you could ask for, the most likable hound a boy could have. He didn't seem to have a mean bone in him. But, Blue--he was a killer, an instinctive killer. Whether a coon or an argumentative male pup, Blue knew only one hold--the throat. His jaws would clamp down on the jugular and he would pin his adversary to the ground. No amount of scratching or clawing could move him.

It was soon over. Blue always won.

That was Blue. A Gary Cooper kind of hound, like the hero in a Zane Grey novel. He never provoked a fight and was slow to become provoked. But I never saw him start a fight or fight a lady. Everybody should have a dog like Blue to remember.

### River Of Used To Be

The hound bawls again. Shakes me back to 1962.

I know that hound is on the end of a chain, but I can't help wanting to follow him down a holler. Season opens in a couple of months. First frost could come in a month. That time of year to follow the bawl of the hounds will soon be here. Yet, it will never be here. Not the time I remember. I'll go hunting again. But, the time of my remembrances will not return.

Ol' Babe, Kate, Blue--they're gone. So are the moonlit bottoms and woodland hills.

Too many houses, too few coon. Too many people who don't understand the call of the hounds.

The coonhound bawls, long and low, the song drifitng in my window. It awakens not so much a desire to follow the hounds, but a yearning to return to the days when I did.

## Keeping Cool

Air conditioning, when I was a boy, was a "Zero" fan humming on the chest-of-drawers.

Windows in the house were open, gauze curtains brushed aside like a bride's veil by any breeze that wafted by. Mud daubers and paper wasps buzzed against window screens.

Tall oaks on the south and west helped break the afternoon sun. Cold water from the well quenched our thirst, the same cold water that cooled the evening milk.

A dip in the creek down the road doused the heat and the sweat from a day in the hay, assuring us a good night's sleep.

It was hot, but having no air conditioning, we

## Jim Hamilton

became acclimated to the heat. We found relief in the scant breeze of a little fan, its hum as much as its air lulling us to sleep.

We didn't have to be neat and clean. There was no disgrace in our sweat. We seldom went anywhere except to the store for a few sacks of feed where other folks dripped just the same as we.

My first encounter with air conditioning was in the supermarket. Its icy blast chilled me just inside the door, and its sultry absence melted me when I left.

I never cared for air conditioning, and I never missed it until we had it in our home. That was the same year I bought my first car with air conditioning--1978.

Air conditioning is the opiate of a society addicted to antiperspirants and appearances of hygiene. Were it not for the modern social convention of always looking neat and dry, as well as smelling nice, I could do without it.

God gave us air conditioning, the world's first evaporative coolers. Polite circles call it perspiration. I call it sweat.

But sweat, however natural and efficient, is not socially acceptable or proper. Even television commercials warn, "Don't let 'em see you sweat!"

Sweat makes shirts cling to the small of your back, burns your eyes, and drips from the end of your nose. Even if you don't mind, folks around you do.

So, to please others more than ourselves, we have air conditioning. Drugged on its menthol ectasy, we retreat from summer heat into our cool cocoons, doors and windows sealed against the heat, and one another.

In the days before air conditioners droned louder than crickets on a warm summer evening, folks would sit outside, swinging on front porches or in their yards watching the stars.

Neighbors visited across the backyard fence, or when they came to call, just shouted through the screen door, "Anybody home?"

We would open the screen and a wasp would fly out. Through open windows we heard the roosters crow, cows bawling for their calves, and 'coon dogs baying at a red squirrel playing outside their pen.

Over the steady hum of an electric fan, we enjoyed lemonade or tea, talked about fishing, and never suspected we lacked a thing--least of all air conditioning.

## Milking Cows

Dairy farming is important to Dallas County, Missouri. It always has been.

Years before four-wheeled pickups rutted fields, before big round bales were stacked in the corners, before tall steel silos were called "blue tombstones," before government buyouts, sell-outs and cop-outs became more important than the kind of hay you fed, folks milked cows and sold the milk.

It was "dairy farming" then too. But in contrast to the farming of today, it was agriculture of another era. Growing up in the 1950s and 1960s, I remember when dairy farming was a way of life for most families up and down our road. It was a business--had to be, to some extent. But, it was more than that. It seems small dairy farms, with cans carried to the road each morning, were as naturally a part of the landscape as cedar trees in the fence rows and meadowlarks perched on rusty barbed

## Jim Hamilton

wire.

I grew up with milk cows. Those big-eyed gentle Jerseys were as much a part of my first eighteen years as any single thing I can remember. Through the years I lived in different houses, went to different schools, and made different friends. But as constant and unchanging as my parents, brothers, and Christmas were the Jersey cows. Even when we didn't milk any, it seems I was always around them.

Dad was an artificial inseminator in the pioneering days of that technique. I was his shadow. During my first nine years I saw the inside of more milk barns than most folks see in a lifetime.

Many were dirt-floored structures, built of rough-sawn native oak, warped and weathered gray. Where the sunlight pierced through cracks between the boards, it sliced a dusty haze that always seemed to smell of old hay, manure and musty straw. Today when I'm in a dairy barn, I feel like a stranger.

In elevated milking parlors laced with plastic and stainless steel pipes, digital lights flash on glass weigh jars, and black and white cows enter wearing electronic devices around their necks to communicate with the computer, which will ration them dairy feed. And in another room, a computer printer spits out a roll of perforated paper telling more than we ever thought we'd want to know about every cow with a transponder on her neck.

No warmth in that kind of barn. Ours was comfortable, hot and dusty in summer, cold and drafty in winter, but as familiar as the kitchen table.

Milking time.

A dozen or so Jersey cows were shut in wooden

## River Of Used To Be

stanchions, the oak two-by-fours worn slick by years of restraining cows anxious to get their grain. Old automobile engine valves dropped through slanted holes to lock the stanchions shut.

Every cow had a name--Radar, Susan, Jester, Heifer, Newy--just like the rest of the family.

We scooped dairy feed from 100-pound burlap bags with a No. 10 can. Two scoops for Radar, three for Susan.

In the loft was sweet-smelling, fine-stemmed lespedeza hay. The leaves shattered and fell to the bottom of the feed trough when we fed lespedeza, looking like oregano, but it was licked clean like molasses sopped with a biscuit from the breakfast plate.

We sat on stools with legs made from persimmon sprouts and oak slabs for the seat, tails invariably wrapped around our necks as we scooted under cows, holding buckets tightly between our knees, and laid our faces against the warm flank. The rhythmic sound of milk squirting into the buckets, steady as a heartbeat, reverberates yet like a tune learned in Sunday School.

Each of us--me, my dad, and brothers--had our own beat, our own music. The buckets, too, were our own, each bent at the top in an oval to fit the grip of our knees.

We carried full buckets of foamy, yellow milk from the barn and poured it into the strainer on top of a tinned milk can. What the Kendall strainer pad didn't filter out, we figured processing or nature would.

We had two kinds of cans, those with flat lids, like mushrooms, the best kind for sitting on when dad gave us hair cuts, and the other kind, which fit down inside the neck of the can and had a crossbar for a

## Jim Hamilton

handle.

Milk had to be cooled in summer. A tub of cool water from the well did the job. Beside the strainer and buckets hung a milk stirrer, sort of an inverted stainless steel frisbee on the end of a long shaft bent to form a handle at the top. Milk had to be stirred to cool quickly.

To keep it overnight, we slipped a burlap bag over the can and soaked it down. It soaked up the water from the tub, and as the water evaporated the milk was kept cool, just as sweat cooled us in summer. After a few years, we got a refrigerated can cooler. Sometimes, I think, we even plugged it in.

In those days, dairy farming ended at the road. We carried the cans to the end of the drive to be picked up by the milk hauler, who loaded them in a square crackerbox of a bed with racks to hold the cans in place.

Maybe it's because I understood dairy farming from a youngster's perspective that farming seemed so simple then. We didin't seem as concerned about government programs, subsidies, and politics. Or, at least, I wasn't. Good cows, good feed, and taking care of both were more important.

The main strategy was to work hard. It didn't seem there were many problems sweat couldn't overcome.

But, as simple as it seemed, my world was insulated from political and enconomic factors which were steadily erasing our traditional farm lifestyle.

I was gone when Dad finally quit milking in the 1970s. Government regulations put him and thousands of other Grade C producers out of business. Dairy farming as we knew it died.

It may have been killed, or it may have just

passed away. Either way, milking cows as a simple way of life is gone, but not forgotten, as long as the old milk strainer still hangs in Dad's barn.

# Owls

The crisp air of a winter night carries upon silent shoulders its denizens' howls, the sharp-edged chilling cacophony of a pack of coyotes, the distant "ar-roo" of a hound on the trail, and the mystic queries of the owl, "whoo-whoo-ha-whoo."

I had stepped onto the back porch to get a stick of wood. The chill air braced my bare shoulders as the storm door slapped behind me, shutting out the lights, noises and stuffy warmth of the house.

It had stopped snowing just after dark, and the fields around the house lay under a dimly-lit blanket of white flannel. The dying wind whistled faintly through the window screen, at first the only sound I heard.

Suddenly my breath was frozen and my ears tuned to a muffled "whoo-whoo" from a distant treeline, followed by a responding call from a closer stand of timber.

Something in that soft "whoo-whoo-ha-whoo" seemed to awaken primal instincts, stirred the smoldering soul of the elemental man, called the spirit from prehistoric fires and into the cover of night.

It had been a long time since I had heard a hoot owl from my back porch. Its call reached not only into my elemental being, but into a storehouse of childhood memories.

I've always been fascinated by owls. Their calls

## Jim Hamilton

have often stopped me in mid-step. As a youngster I was drawn outside to attend the symphonic exchange of hoot owls in our woods and the big woods across the road. Sometimes six or eight owls would answer back and forth, the closest just a hundred yards or so away in the corner of our woods. Their calls were like soft music.

Less soothing were the bloodcurdling screams of the screech owls in our woods. I recall vividly an encounter with one of these tiny cousins to a hoot owl when I was eleven or twelve years old.

The ground was blanketed with snow, and the air cold. Low clouds shut out any light from the heavens that night, and the landscape was dark, save the house and barn lights. I had taken my sled, an orange crate wired to its back, into the woods to bring up a load of firewood. Tugging the loaded sled back down an old logging trail, I was stopped in my snowy tracks by the sudden scream of a screech owl no more than ten feet above my head. I knew instantly what it was, but was startled, nonetheless.

I shined my flashlight into the low branches of a large post oak, and there he sat on a large limb near the trunk, glaring at me with large round eyes. He didn't fly, but just wanted me to know he was there. It was my first close look at a screech owl. The animal itself was much less intimidating than its scream. As I tugged my sled out of the woods and into the barnlot, I heard him scream a shrill "good riddance."

In my growing-up years I heard and saw plenty of hoot owls (really barred owls, I think) and screech owls. They were as common as cottontail rabbits.

Less ordinary was the huge owl we encountered one night while coon hunting across the road. It was

# River Of Used To Be

some thirty years ago. We were working our way back to the house after a fruitless hunt, walking up a broad draw in the timber. We heard the heavy flapping of its wings before it flew through the circle of our lantern's light, looking for an instant like a phantom, a white apparition with wings three or four feet across. As quickly as we saw it, it was gone. We knew it was no ordinary hoot owl. The best we could figure, it was a snowy owl wintering in that woods.

In more recent years I've been intrigued by the mid-day exchange of hoot owls on the ridge just below the U.S. 64 bridge over the Niangua. It's been ten years since I frequented that spot. I don't know if owls still call that ridge home, or if the canoes of summer have sent them to more remote ridges.

Wherever and whenever heard, as dusk darkens the river bottom, or in the cold, crisp air of a winter night, the soft "whoo-whoo-ha-whoo" of the owl still reaches deep into the primal soul. Native Americans both revered and feared the owl. It has a place in Indian legends as both the messenger of evil and the gatekeeper of eternity.

I don't know which I believe. Maybe neither. Yet, the owl's call awakens prehistoric instincts, urging we leave the fire, and become one with the night.

## Last of the Good Old Days

Another generation of seniors rehearses for their final high school assignment--graduation.

It seems so long ago I wore my mortar board and flowing gown down the long aisle and up to the stage

## Jim Hamilton

where we sat on metal folding chairs, sweating under late May's humidity and the clammy tension of that night. The class of '65.

Fair Grove, Missouri, 1965. The last of the Good Old Days.

Drugs were something we heard about but never saw. Hippies smoked pot in California. We saw it on TV, but it was all a fantasy to us, like Superman or Huckleberry Hound.

Innocent years. The Beatles still sang silly love songs, and kids were sent home from school for letting their hair grow as long as that of John, Paul, Ringo, or George.

Vietnam meant a toddling war in a country somewhere between Africa and Japan. We paid little heed to that monster child with an appetite that would soon claim some of our lives.

Johnson's Great Society was being built while Ladybird was tearing down highway billboards. Blacks were still fighting slavery in the South, but up in Fair Grove, we didn't have the slightest idea why. We were an ignorant bunch, but happily so. There was so much we didn't even care to know.

There was not nearly as much as we had to know. We'd never heard of microchips, bits, bytes, or computers of any sort, except for "electronic brains." Nobody ever mentioned AIDS, and "safe sex" meant married. Only doctors knew about cholesterol. Light beer was the fake stuff they drank on TV. Rap music was a scratched record, and a transistor radio was the closest anyone ever came to a boom box. Besides, we wanted them in our pockets, not on our shoulders.

Compared to us, these grads today are pretty

smart.

But, we knew something in '65 these kids can't begin to understand--we knew our commitment to Uncle Sam.

We all had to reckon with the draft.

The draft. Whether we were into the service or not, it shaped all our lives. All jobs were temporary for a man classified 1-A. His life was on hold, in limbo, floating around in the Twilight Zone.

It made us different from succeeding generations. We knew the long arm and steel grip of Uncle Sam on the napes of our necks.

It's something these grads may not understand, but for the young men in the Class of '65 it was a fact. As our eighteenth birthdays neared, the reality grew clearer. Like it or not, childhood was coming to an end.

Ignorance and innocence were sweet, but brief, for the Class of '65.


## River of Used To Be

I drove past Potter's Ford last Wednesday and stopped at the old catfishing hole.

That piece of river, like so many others along the Pomme de Terre, harbors many cherished childhood memories. But it wasn't as I remembered it. I walked out on the gravel bar which filled the river to its middle, and looked over my shoulder at an old maple tree some twenty feet behind me.

As a boy I used to sit on the dirt bank and cast around that old tree. Where I stood Wednesday was, back then, ten feet deep. It was a good cast across the

## Jim Hamilton

old catfishing hole. Today, it's hardly a good spit. To look at it now--a shallow stream you could wade across most anywhere--you'd hardly believe this once was a river of deep, roiling fishing holes like the one which yielded fat bullheads some thirty or more years ago.

But it's not just the river that's changed. The dirt road to the river is now paved, and the riverbank where this boy escaped from time to time with his dad and brothers is now just a hooligan's party place.

The fishing hole belongs to another time. Yet, in the timeless dimensions of eternity, there, on a warm summer night, Dad, Russell, and I sit on the bank watching our poles by kerosene lantern light, listening to the muskrats paddle across the slough, catching catfish until the moon climbs over the ridge.

In a dimension unbounded by time, this youngster still rambles up and down that river, his footprints forever left in the river's shifting gravel bar and sand.

And from their eternal resting places above the river on a green and pleasant ridge, a girl of nineteen and a boy of twenty-one join the boyhood spirits of their father and brother at the river's edge.

Summer nights, in truth or dream, you'll find we three in conversation deep down at the old fishing hole-- forever young, forever free, rambling the rivers and ridges of the Pomme de Terre that used to be.

# Part Two

# GRANDMA'S ROSES

## Home and Family

## Grandma's Roses

In my mother's yard are yellow roses.

Old-fashioned roses, with spindly, stickery vines that reach out and grab Dad's overalls as he walks past them to his truck.

Prolific vines, spreading in a widening circle from the first planting in the old yard fence row. At times they're a nuisance.

Until they blossom.

Brilliant yellow, the profuse flowers bend the willowy vines in bright arches that bow to the ground under a heavy dew.

They are Grandma Daly's roses.

Delicate, lacy roses, with thin petals piled like yellow petticoats.

An elegant Victorian lady's roses.

In my mother's yard, her mother's roses.

Grandma Daly has been gone for many years. Yet, she is with us still. She is the beautiful Victorian lady in the photograph on our hallway wall, and in the roses that bloom each spring in my mother's yard.

Someday the old photograph, like my memories of her, will dim. But the yellow roses will not.

Undisturbed, they will flourish and grow, and untold generations will yet enjoy Grandma's yellow roses. They will bend to lift the sagging vines, clip the delicate flowers, brush the dew from velvety petals, and prick their fingers on the stickery vines.

### Jim Hamilton

They will not know these are Grandma's roses. But, Grandma Daly's roses will bloom for them just the same.

Throughout these Ozarks we see each spring on brushy corners, in greening pastures, on long overgrown lots, and around crumbling, ancient homesteads, orderly rows of daffodils raising their yellow trumpets. "Grandma's flowers," in these long-deserted, vacant spots, heritage lovingly nurtured generations ago, left for eternity to enjoy.

We don't often know whose grandma's flowers they are. But, like Grandma Daly's roses, they blossom for us just the same.

Roses, daffodils, lilac bushes, and tiger lilies, flowers of every sort. The bright warm heritage of grandmothers all.

## Grandma Never Watched TV

Grandma Daly never had a TV.

Even in what broadcasting now calls the "Golden Age" of live TV, Grandma Daly never had a television set. At least none that I can recall.

She seemed to manage life well enough without it, even in her winter years. She had quite enough to see and hear without the omnipresent blare of a television set.

She had a grand old radio and stacks of newspapers, as well as grandchildren.

As I recall my sapling days, Grandma Daly was never wanting for occupation. She had me to keep her busy, and when I wasn't around, Grandpa and his sign

## River Of Used To Be

shop were plenty to stave off any threat of boredom. Besides, there was always plenty of work to be done.

If we were to eat, there was cookwood to split. Grandma Daly cooked every meal on an old wood stove, though a perfectly good gas range stood in the corner, starving for attention.

Grandma Daly was a Victorian lady, with nineteenth century ways. Old photos reveal her classic beauty--delicate features framed by a high collar and long hair piled in a stately bun. She was a lady of highest class, irrespective of station.

A pioneer child, she traveled with her mother in a two-wheeled cart from Washington state to Minnesota; a bold journey for a woman and child alone across the tortuous Rocky Mountains and expansive Great Plains. What, in her winter years, could a television bring to compare with that adventure of her early spring?

What Grandma Daly did without TV was lots of important grandma things. She rocked children in her squeaky old rocking chair in the kitchen. She cooked and mended. She made wild cherry jelly when I picked the cherries. She took me downtown on the city bus, walked me over to Doling Park, gave me Indian head pennies and red and green plastic mills. She dug through countless musty drawers and boxes digging out marvelous things to keep me entertained.

Religiously, she saved cardboard dividers from shredded wheat boxes for the Indian lore they bore, and helped me find all the right stuff to make war bonnets and arrows, and drums from oatmeal boxes and pieces of inner tube.

And she always made sure ginger snap cookies were in good supply.

# Jim Hamilton

Grandma Daly taught me how to drink green tea and eat sliced tomatoes covered in sugar. She introduced me to rock candy, and let me use time-blackened paring knives to peel apples picked from the huge tree in her back yard.

When my belly ached, she once gave me a syrupy hot toddy, and her own aches she doctored with pungent camphorated liniment.

Long before *Sesame Street* used TV to educate in inventive ways, Grandma Daly taught me to read and write before I was five. Campbell's Soup cans and cracker boxes were my texts and the kitchen table was my desk where I copied labels carefully, down to every graphic swirl. My classroom was my store of fruits, vegetables, and other empty cans, each opened on the bottom side, washed clean, and stacked in orange crate shelves. A storekeeper had to know how to read all the labels. Among those empty cans, my favorite was always the Log Cabin Syrup's tin cabin. The chimney was the pouring spout.

Despite the lack of TV, Grandma also guided me through several chapters of history, with stacks of sepia Sunday supplement tabloids from World War II, telling of the exploits and victories of our boys oversees, and from old copies of *Look* and *Life* hoarded for more than a decade under her bed.

A million things my Grandma taught me, but she never told me to turn on or turn off the TV.

These days it's hard to imagine a home without a TV, where old folks and children enjoy one another's company, and together find entertainment.

As I recall those softly focused days of Grandma Daly's winter years and my sapling spring, I can't help

# River Of Used To Be

but wonder if we wouldn't all be better served by fewer TV's and more Grandma Dalys in their place.

## Mother's Days

Mother's Day is Sunday, a time which evokes visions of motherly stereotypes and drives sons and daughters to pen lines of embarrassingly gushy prose. But I have a somewhat different thought as this Mother's Day approaches.

Mom, as I recall, devoted most of her younger years to buying potatoes and pork chops to feed a hungry crowd--four strapping sons and their dad--who watched from the barn for her car headlights each night.

She brought our daily bread home in grocery sacks, and what she didn't spend on food for us might have gone for a little extra hay.

Spent it all, you see, so her boys would have a better place to be than on some city street corner or juvenile pool-shooter's den of iniquity.

While she worked in town those many years over vials of ruby-red and blackened blood, peering through microscopes for errant cells, persimmon sprouts fell before our double-bladed axes, and the udders of Jersey milk cows yielded to calloused hands.

We grew strong on that brushy thirty-nine acres, the briars we piled and burned etching character and discipline into our souls, though at the time we didn't know it.

Now, a lot of good might be written of moms, ours and others alike.

But tonight, as the oil burns late, the one thing I

recall as most important of all is not what she made us do, the pies she baked, or any of that silly, mushy stuff, but simply that her dedication allowed us the freedom to be just boys growing up on a few hardscrabble acres of Dallas County farm.

## Dad's Day

It's that time of the year again, that time when Dad gets his annual issue of socks, underwear, handkerchiefs, and sure-fire, guaranteed-to-slay 'em fish lures.

Sunday is Father's Day, that once-a-year when we pay due tribute to the cantankerous old man who lives with Mom.

Father's Day has a different meaning for each of us, and each of us expresses our sentiments in different ways because we all have unique relationships with our fathers. But whatever the basis of that relationship--love, respect, companionship, trust, understanding, money, a '57 Chevy, or whatever--most of us have a special feeling for Dad.

But there's no point in getting mushy about it. All the good things we might say about Dad he knows anyway. Just ask him.

All we can really say is that Dad is just Dad. Each of us knows what that means and there's not much more to say that couldn't be said just as well with a package of plastic worms.

Dads come in assorted sizes, shapes, complexions, and temperaments; no two are alike.

Sometime or another we may have come across

## River Of Used To Be

a model we liked a little better than the one we got, but it's hard to imagine a dad different from the one we have.

We all went though those ages when we thought Dad was pretty-near perfect, and then later about as imperfect as a man could get, until we finally realized that he is a little of both and we're not much different. The only perfect fathers we'll ever see are the ones on television.

It's hard to contemplate fatherhood for very long without conjuring visions of Fred MacMurray leaning back in a recliner, smoking a pipe, and reading the evening paper in his perfect, all-male household.

As the perfect father on television's **My Three Sons**, MacMurray epitomized all that was desirable in fatherly behavior and decorum. An aviation engineer living in a nice suburb of Perfectly Middle Class USA, he was the perfect provider.

Do you ever recall Chip going to school with a hole in the knee of his Levis, or Uncle Charley reaching far to the back of the cupboard for the last box of macaroni and cheese?

MacMurray was a page cut from a Sears and Roebuck catalog, relaxing with pipe in mouth and examining blueprints for a new airplane. Regardless of interruption or provocation to anger, he was never angry. He never yelled or stomped or cussed when the family car came back with a crumpled fender. He never took the boys to the woodshed, and he never seemed to be wrong about anything. His judgement was that of Solomon.

In the midst of chaos, he was a tranquilizing patriarch in a casual sweater with leather patches on the elbows, encircled in clouds of Sir Walter Raleigh aromatic blend.

He was perfectly unbelievable, but the kind of father needed to rear his nearly perfect children.

An earlier perfect father, of course, was Robert Young on *Father Knows Best*. And he always did.

That was the era of pefect parents on the miraculous boob tube. Who could fault Timmie's father on *Lassie*, or be critical of whatever his name was on *The Donna Reed Show* or doubt the wisdom of Robert Reed on *The Brady Bunch*?

But, as each of us compares our own dads to those celluloid creations, it is easy to see that Hollywood was wrong, and our own imperfect fathers came a lot nearer to filling the bills than those film dads.

With one exception, perhaps. There was one cantankerous daddy on television who seemed more like the real thing--Walter Brennan of *The Real McCoys*.

But none of us would admit our own fathers bear any similarities to that old man.

Now Grandpa?

Perhaps.

## A House Too Quiet

The house is too quiet tonight as I sit at the table and try to write.

No Jazzy Jeff or Paula Abdul to rock my concentration. No MTV or Downtown Julie Brown. The house is much too quiet tonight.

No sisters arguing, footsteps tromping, or bedroom doors squeaking shut. No voices lilting on the air

# River Of Used To Be

in the back. It's a silence some folks might like, but for the likes of me it's much too quiet.

Abandoned and forlorn on the corner of the desk, the unexpectant telephone sits silent. Rooms at each end of the hall are unlit. The beds are made and the curtains straight.

The girl have gone to camp and taken with them the music, noise, lights, and energy that shake this dreary house when they're around.

They're not here tonight and it's awfully quiet. Even the dogs don't bark; no one to listen. Shadows of the future fall, I fear, in the silent corners of this house.

The gravity with which the silence falls on this couple's graying heads foreshadows the quieter years I fear ahead.

The house is much too quiet tonight, too quiet to write.

Lay down my pen. Turn out the light.

## A Hole In The House

There's a hole in our house, a dark, yawning pit, an ancient cistern, a black abyss at the end of the hall.

Our daughter has gone to college. Such a little girl. Amazing that her absence leaves such a fathomless void.

From in my chair at the brink of its gaping jaws, I stare into her empty, silent room, the bed neatly made, hardwood floor bare and clean, emptiness filling its corners like darkness fills the night.

Sunday was moving day, no time for silly sentiments. Too many boxes to be lugged.

# Jim Hamilton

The day started in a frenzy of prodding and last-minute packing to beat the afternoon crush of other students and their families. I had loaded the pickup the previous evening. All that was needed was for Angela to throw herself and a few clothes in her car. At least, that's all I thought there was to it. I'll never understand. I've never worn makeup or curled my hair.

When finally we left, our vehicles bristled with more goods than Steinbeck's Okies hauled to California.

Heaps of personal treasures cluttered the busy sidewalk outside the dormitory where an army of sweating fathers and fretting mothers unloaded their babies' necessities.

Ours was soon added to the clutter and we joined in the diligent, groaning file like worker ants carrying crumbs from a picnic table. Plastic crates, more than a dozen boxes of shoes, a small refrigerator, a typewriter, bags of books, boxes and boxes of stuff--all lugged up to the fourth floor. I didn't count the trips, but the sweat could have been measured in gallons.

Yet, the toughest chore was not the dozens of trips up four flights of stairs. It was the leaving, but none of us could quite admit it in the bustle and excitement of moving.

We just left her there, lots of unpacking yet to do, worn out and cranky the same as we. We just left her there and there she remains. We are back home, our lives not much specifically changed but for the hole in our house, that gaping, dark hole.

I didn't notice its size at first; its dimensions become more profound at night when her car's familiar hum never crosses the driveway.

I want to wait up as I have so many, many nights,

# River Of Used To Be

but now have no reason to.

This is for what she was born nearly nineteen years ago when her mother and I, too, were young and far from our families and home, to ultimately leave and etch out a life all her own. I'm sure in my mind that she's doing fine.

But that doesn't diminish the emptiness of the vacant room.

From this day the abyss will always exist. The child who left will never return the same child to her childhood home.

## Magnetic Tapestry

We're gonna have to get a new refrigerator. This old green one is too small.

It's not that the freezer won't hold enough ice cream and pizza, that nothing more can be crammed on the shelves. It's the door: We are running out of places to stick refrigerator magnets.

We've talked about getting a new refrigerator, but this avocado green one matches our stove and we don't need a new stove. Stove door magnets never quite caught on like the freezer door variety.

They tell me no one makes avocado green appliances these days, so we would never find a match for the stove, not that it would matter much. Our magnets would cover most of any color refrigerator door.

Some folks keep scrapbooks or diaries. We just buy refrigerator magnets.

I can imagine what a puzzle our magnetic menagerie might pose for archeologists some thousands

# Jim Hamilton

of years from now. The mysteries of the Rosetta Stone would pale in contrast. But, like that and other mysteries of antquity, refrigerator magnets make perfect sense in present context. They are, in essence, a journal of our wanderings. Magnetic states chart more recent trips-- Iowa, Missouri, Arkansas, Oklahoma, Texas, New Mexico, Arizona, Utah, Colorado, Kansas, Nebraska, Wyoming, and South Dakota.

Seagulls perched on pencil-sized pier posts recall a trip to Seattle. Plastic ladybugs are family heirlooms, as are plastic peaches, pears, and bananas.

Magnetic locomotives from Chama, New Mexico, and Silverton, Colorado, steam toward a ceramic tile Buffalo from somewhere I can't recall.

A sandpainted Indian rides his pony toward a Mesa Verde license plate, and Old Glory waves beside a macrame Granny Smith apple.

McDonald's spans the turnpike, and Christ of the Ozarks towers over a pewter bison from South Dakota.

Ribbon fish swim among gingham butterflies, while a zesty jalapeno tempts Tweety Bird and Sylvester the Cat. Like a Norman tapestry, the door's details unfold. The longer you look, the more you see, the more personal history is recalled.

Some images bitter, some sweet, each magnetic piece is a panel in a tapestry still upon the loom.

## House That Was A Home

We are leaving this house which has been our home for a dozen years.

In just a few days these walls which have echoed

## River Of Used To Be

the laughter and cries of our daughters will welcome another generation of playful voices.

As houses go, this has been no uncommon structure--just a solid, but simple sanctuary from winter cold, summer heat, spring tempests, and the dark of night.

Those things it might have done for anyone. Yet, for us it has been home, the harbor of our hearts.

Though we leave it now, this house will, in our mind's eye, always be a place of countless warm memories, of many happy times, as well as days of unrelenting darkness.

This has been our children's home. It was in this house that Angela grew from Barbie dolls to high school proms. And it is the memories of her room, I confess, that make this house most difficult to leave. . . until I walk through that familiar door and realize the room is gone, existing now only in spirit and memory, just as Angela does in eternity.

Melissa grew here from pedalling Hot Wheels on the carport to learning to guide the family wheels onto that same concrete slab.

Memories fill this place like faint perfume, or the distant laughter of little girls. As I walk from door to door, warm images of the past fill the vacant rooms:

\* Reading Melissa one of Kipling's ***Just So Stories***, then tucking her in under a Strawberry Shortcake quilt and kissing every one of her dolls and stuffed animals goodnight before I could turn out the light.

\* Watching the light under the door to Angela's room long after it should have been out, opening it to find her fast asleep, her Bible folded open over her

# Jim Hamilton

chest.
  * Our families gathered around the kitchen table at Thanksgiving, kids sitting on a piano bench at a card table in the living room.
  * A nervous boyfriend at the back door, and the same young man fidgeting on the couch while waiting for Angela to put the final touches to her hair.
  * Slumber parties in the basement family room, where a half-dozen little girls giggled and whispered in sleeping bags well into the night.
  * Tinsel on the front room rug, joyous Christmas mornings with gifts too numerous to count, and mountains of wrapping paper at little girls' feet.
  * The wading pool in the back yard, with as many buckets of toys as water in it, Melissa splashing Angela while she was working on her tan.

  Memories. Soft and warm, they drift through this house like dust on Autumn sunlight.
  Yet, these rooms which echoed the happy voices of little girls at play, now harbor memories of less happy days.
  The walls stand as they always have, but the warmth of their shelter is gone. This home of a dozen years is again just a house. Cardboard boxes are packed and stacked in every room. Our season in this house is nearly through.
  This week we move to another just outside of town, in a new season, we pray, a place to become our home anew.

# Part Three

# GOD OWNS THE WOODS

## Places, People, and Diversions

## My Woods

I have a few acres of trees and brush I call my woods. I love going to the woods. I like its trees. I like them most of all because they are mine. I can cut them down if I want. More importantly, I can let them stand.

I prefer the woods, though not so much as a place to own as a place to be. Ownership of pieces of the earth, after all, is a fragile thing, an abstract concept that some cultures can scarcely comprehend. We are stewards, users and abusers.

God owns the woods. He may actually live there.

I love the woods not so much for its trees, but for what I can't hear and see. Not so much for what is there, but for what isn't. No telephone, no radio, no MTV, no mailbox, no front door, no VDT.

Nobody.

A treeless prairie would serve the same purpose, with waves of tallgrass rippling like suntanned shoulders beneath a broad Nebraska sky.

The prairie, too, would be a nice place to be, as long as there was no one there but me, those times when the earth and sky are my favorite company.

Times like those in my woods.

## Fourth of July at Long Lane

Like a big slice of watermelon, juice and seeds dripping from the chin of a freckle-faced youngster, the Fourth of July at Long Lane, Missouri, paints a portrait of grass roots Americans enjoying their holiday.

The evening chores behind them, the frantic holiday rush stilled by the warm evening air, folks come to the Long Lane Community Park each Fourth of July

## Jim Hamilton

in a relaxed celebration.

They come for supper, sitting at long tables enjoying the tender barbecued chicken--chicken so well done it falls off the bone and melts like smoke on the palate.

They come to be entertained, unfolding lawn chairs around the dance pavilion, listening to country tunes played by local musicians. Some folks dance a square or two. Many just watch. Most of all, they just come to relax with friends and neighbors.

The Fourth of July at Long Lane is just a big family reunion, where relatives are joined by common customs, concerns, and ideas, if not by blood.

Neighbors and relatives lean across the arms of their folding chairs to swap stories of drought, fishing trips, horses they've sold or steers they've raised, and remark on how much the kids have grown since the last time they saw them.

The kids run around as they would in their own backyards, and hardly anyone notices or worries.

The food, music, and visiting go on until the first star begins to glimmer. Folks move their chairs downhill, towards their cars and trucks, to watch the big fireworks display. Aerial blasts draw exclamations of appreciation from the crowd, especially the kids. Too soon for them, the fireworks are spent and the evening is over.

The relaxed mood of the previous hours is broken by the rumble of engines and the glare of headlights. The park is left silent and empty save for the paper cups and plates that never made it to the trash can, a stray poster tossed by the night breeze, the lingering acrid black powder smoke, and the memories of another Fourth of July at Long Lane.

# River Of Used To Be

## Rivers

A river is a mystery.

A contradiction, it's a haunting, primordial mystery where dark waters slow and creep along a murky, muddy bottom known only to the whiskers of catfish and the armored bellies of turtles. Then-- sparkling-bright champagne, chortling like an oriole across a calico shallow of gravel, where silver-scaled minnows tickle a toddler's toes.

The river was meant for men to fish in.

God, in all his wisdom, saw fit to make rivers, then fish, then men, to whom he granted dominion over the rivers, and the fish.

Men know it. The fish don't

Men made lakes to fish in, to float big boats, to give water skiers room to turn around on, and for bass tournaments.

They made all this out of rivers. To improve on God's handiwork, thinking themselves wiser than he, I suppose.

In these Ozarks, I prefer the rivers. From the banks of a river I engage in an ancient form of fishing, maybe the purest form of fishing.

With a casting pole and reel, I tie on a hook and sinker, string a worm on the hook, and plunk it out in a likely-looking spot. And sit.

Anything might bite. Worms are natural bait for virtually every fish in the river, from carp to trout.

Whatever bites, I'll take it.

Maybe nothing will bite. Still-fishing on the river bottom is an exercise in relaxation.

I throw my worm where I think the fish might be,

then wait for them to get there, if the pumpkinseeds and crawdads don't steal my bait first.

Not many folks fish this way anymore. I don't know why. They should. Fish, after all, are not the real objective of fishing trips.

We escape with pole in hand to find quiet and peace, to get away from the hurry and stress.

A stringer of fish reassures us that we haven't wasted the time. We've put food on the table, which is what all the hurrying about is all about in the first place.

Folks don't sit and fish much anymore because they don't know how. Chances are, if you're plugging up the river in a bass boat and you run across someone sitting on the bank, three lines out and poles propped in forked sticks stuck in the ground, chaw of tobacco in his mouth and can of worms by his side, it'll be an old-timer.

Chances are, too, though he may not seem to be hurried, he'll show you a string of fish.

Old-timers are part of the mystery.

# Hometown

The old Buffalo water tower is not coming down.

I got a letter Monday from a former resident that was worried that the old tower, which in her childhood stood like a beacon over Buffalo and welcomed travelers home, was being replaced.

She can be assured that the sixty-six year old water tower will stand for many years to come, and no matter which highway brings her to town, on a clear day she will see it miles ahead of her arrival.

# River Of Used To Be

The only difference now is that she will be guided home by two towers; one to remind her of her childhood home, the other to remind her of the growth and changes in Buffalo since she left.

Our letter writer wrote: "All of us transplanted Missourian's are hungry for news of our old hometown."

Sorry, the old hometown isn't here, at least not as it is remembered.

Hometown is a mythical place where the Fourth of July always means homemade ice cream and grand fireworks, where kindly old men sit in the shade and swap fishing tales, where winters are spent building snow forts and sledding, where haircuts are twenty-five cents and a coke is a nickel.

We would not want Hometown to betray the hearts and fond memories of its citizens, but we who live here are citizens of a living, changing community which resembles Hometown only in its landmarks and mythology.

## Gentle Spirits Of Union Mound

Cemeteries. Storytellers have made them places to fear. To others, though, they are just gardens of stone teetering over rotting bones.

Perhaps they haven't the kindred souls to truly see. These hallowed grounds are like a book to be opened, a family Bible on a table by the rocking chair.

Where most folks see the fields of buried dead, others find communion with the hearts and spirits of their generations past, discover from the names etched in weathered stone the roots of our habitation in their

# Jim Hamilton

Ozarks promised land.

On a wooded ridge just west of Pfeiffer Creek is just such a place--a grassy tree-bordered knoll where the spirits of Dallas County ancestors rest.

More than 150 years ago, before the massive burr oaks were logged from the river bottoms, before the blue-stem prairies were cut into patchwork quilts by roads and fences, Dallas County families entrusted their loved ones to the hard earth of Union Mound. Now, mottled gray stones mark the humble graves of founding generations. Once chalk-white and smooth as the face of a child, the old markers are broken, weathered, and rough to the touch of the palm, wrinkled and spotted like the hands of an old man, their shallow inscriptions all but gone.

Yet, beneath these aged stones lie the bones, in the shade of the trees linger the spirits, of men whose frontier stature casts long shadows across this garden of meandering stones.

There's old Sam, who at thirty-two fought a war in Mexico and at forty-seven took up Union arms, not because he loved to fight, but because he had to do in his life those things necessary of a man.

Then there's Absalom. He came to these parts with his family from North Carolina in 1839. In 1847, he fought in the Mexican War, a mounted dragoon guarding the Santa Fe Trail. He was in the first company of soldiers raised in Dallas County. The celebration on their return was legendary. Old-timers told of whole beeves being roasted and barrels of whiskey consumed. It was good to have the young men home.

Young Eddie saw unspeakable horrors far from his gentle Ozarks home. A Union soldier in the Confed-

## River Of Used To Be

Confederate prison at Andersonville, Georgia, he was one of the lucky few who survived. He was twenty-one at the end of the war. Doubtless, the memories would haunt him for another seventy-one years. He died in 1936 at age ninety-two, and rests now in the shaded corner of Union Mound.

The cemetery is quiet this morning, but for the steady beat of a light rain in the trees along its edge. The stones speak silent volumes of history, the flowering bushes planted at a soldier father's tomb of the love of those who entrusted to this earth and God his noble soul.

In the deep green shadows below the trees, spirits move on the breeze. In the gentle spring rain, soldiers in dusty uniforms stand with wives in long dresses and barefoot children in home-sewn clothes.

Grandfathers in oft-patched overalls light their pipes and watch me pass, whispering to me with each stone I touch, each hand I hold.

The gentle spirits of Union Mound.


## Thistles

It's dry.

At least it was when I wrote this column. Rain was possible this week, so, as you read this, you might be sitting in your living room surrounded by rusty coffee cans, listening to the cacophonic rhythms of rain: plink, plink, plunk. . . ploink--and chuckling under your drip about this ignorant sonofacoonhunter who can't tell the difference between a drought and a forty-year flood.

It's a gamble, but I'll risk it.

# Jim Hamilton

It sure is dry.

Yards are curling and gardens have to be watered or they wither. Just doesn't seem to be a growing green thing that prospers in this kind of weather. . . except one. Musk thistles are doing great.

Their healthy purple heads bob defiantly in the June breeze, decorating the right-of-way along highways and country roads, bounding across river bottoms and untilled ridges like fuzzy lilac ping-pong balls on thorny stilts.

It doesn't seem to take much to make a musk thistle plant prosper, except ignorance and neglect.

Ignorance is great for propagation. As long as folks are ignorant of the harm a single seedhead can do, we're going to see many more musk thistles flourishing.

Neglect makes great fertilizer. Thistles can take over a field and spread to the neighbor's fields. Neglect 'em, and you might as well be hauling manure to them. All a musk thistle really needs to be happy and prolific is to be left alone.

They're stickery devils. With thousands of airborne seeds, they spread like prairie fire. Musk thistles are on Missouri's noxious weed list; it's against the law to let them grow on your land.

But, they sure are pretty.

Somewhere, I'm sure, is a little old gardener with a plot of yucca plants, prickly pear, devil's walking stick, and horse nettle. And smack dab in the middle of all that is his pride and joy: the finest specimen of purple-crowned musk thistle you ever imagined. Carefully nurtured, watered, and the weeds thinnned out.

And, he's as proud of those prickly plants as a Dutch maid is of her tulip patch.

# River Of Used To Be

Sometimes, when I drive around this countryside in June, I'd swear there are a lot of folks who must think those purple flowers are real pretty. Might even find some of them in fluted vases on coffee tables in their homes.

## Buttered Toast

Went out to eat breakfast the other day. I went because I was hungry, but I could see right away that was the wrong reason.

Breakfast is not necessarily a meal, but more a time of day from about 7:00 a.m. to nearly noon or sometimes later, when the good ol' boys and other regulars gather at the cafes and coffee shops for daily fellowshippin'.

The hash brown potatoes may have been sopped in yesterday's bacon renderings, the over easy eggs neither over nor easy, the sausage freezer-burned and stale as if it had been cooked all the previous afternoon on the hood of a four-wheel drive Ford, and all of it two days coming out. But it doesn't matter.

Food is secondary to the fellowshippin'. (I use the term fellowshippin', normally associated with religious gatherings, because the regulars are pretty religious about their breakfast.)

If you can't take the atmosphere with the breakfast, then you might as well go get yourself a McMuffin, because it's the same all over.

Now I've eaten breakfast in a lot of greasy spoons, from places that pretended to be something they weren't to places that didn't pretend to be much good

## Jim Hamilton

and remained true to their reputations.

Buffalo's eateries generally offer pretty good fare in comparison to their counterparts. Better than most, by far. But, I don't know how they score on a calendar scale. I never paid attention.

Bill Trogdon (aka William Least-Heat Moon) classified cafes in his book *Blue Highways* by the number of calendars on their walls. A four-calendar restaurant, for example, he figured was a top-notch place to eat.

I have a less sophisticated system. I put restaurants in two categories: Those that serve butter and those that don't.

I don't like margarine.

I realize that corn growers have to make a profit just the same as dairy farmers; that doesn't have a thing to do with it. I just don't like margarine. I especially don't like my toast brushed or rolled with melted down margarine before it's ever carried to my table.

For all I know, the "buttered" toast is the product of some guy in the back with a spray gun and a barrel of Mazola corn oil.

I don't like my toast oiled. I like it buttered.

I like butter on bread, toast, hot rolls, corn bread, potatoes, peas, sweet potatoes, and corn-on-the-cob.

Make my fat butterfat.

## Welcome Return To Ozarks

It's good to be back in the Ozarks.

After a circle of more than 2,300 miles to and through New Mexico, the green hills of the Ozarks look mighty hospitable.

## River Of Used To Be

There is a lot of impressive scenery on the Western plains and mountains, but nowhere does the country welcome habitation as it does in the Ozarks. And, our hills and prairies aren't bad to look at, either.

Seems folks from all over the country appreciate them more than we natives do.

From Oklahoma City west, the hospitable nature of the plains declines and it becomes a hard, sometimes barren, country.

The red dirt of western Oklahoma is undoubtedly prosperous to farm, at least for some folks. And the High Plains grasslands of the Texas Panhandle certainly have more promise than the arid brush of New Mexico. I suppose I could make do in the farming and cattle country of western Oklahoma and the Texas Panhandle, but I would always feel like I was just visiting, expecting to return any day to the clear streams, hardwood forests, and enfolding hills of the Missouri Ozarks.

I read somewhere that the Texas Panhandle has the flattest land of anywhere in the United States. I believe it. Rainwater stands in plowed fields because it doesn't know which way to run.

If you had one of those old trucks you had to part on a hill to start every morning, you'd be dead outta luck on much of the Panhandle.

The Jemez Mountains of New Mexico were as appealing as ever. The tall pines, imposing rock, and green meadows of the high mountain valleys present an idyllic scene straight off a drugstore calendar.

The variety of the landscape from desert mesas to meandering trout streams provide a porfolio of idyllic scenes.

However, the harshness of the country is ever

apparent.

There is also the reminder on postcards of winters with four to six feet of snow. The high mountain pastures are cleared of cattle in anticipation of winter's grip, and all but the most hardy residents move to the low country.

Winter in the Ozarks is sometimes tough, but it's tolerable.

In 2,300 miles, we saw mule deer, prairie dogs, pronghorn antelope, Indians of several different tribes, Mexican-Americans, Spanish-Americans, and lots of other species unfamiliar to the Ozarks.

But we never saw a bluetick coonhound. Hard to feel at home anywhere without hounds.

It's good to be back in the Ozarks.

## Windyville Happy Homemakers

I went to Windyville, Missouri, last week to cover the presentation of a state flag to the Happy Homemakers Extension Club.

It was a road Charles Kuralt should have travelled, a winding trek from Buffalo to Windyville, across Benton Branch and Williams Ford, through a wind-tousseled panorama of brilliant fall foliage with only one stop along the way to drag a dead elm tree from the narrow dirt road. It was a road which, on the return, passed that ancient monolith, Lone Rock, and crept cautiously down Dousinberry Branch Hill, scene of many unhappy winter driving episodes.

The Happy Homemakers Club of Windyville meets in the Windyville Community Building, built in

## River Of Used To Be

about 1925. It is a large, white, clapboard building resembling an old schoolhouse. But it is not. Never was.

Inside, from the stamped ceiling, are suspended lights with globes the color of Jersey milk. The plastered walls have been panelled over in recent years. The floor is bare and well-worn wood, to which is fastened several rows of old wooden theater seats. At the front of the room the floor is raised several inches, as is common in church buildings, and, indeed, the structure may once have served religious purposes. The dominant feature, however, is a large, wood-burning stove, set nearly in the center of the room.

Enter the Windyville Community Building and you sense you have stepped backward in time, perhaps into the years before World War II. The ghosts of country folks of generations long gone must dwell contentedly within the warm, wooden walls. You can feel their presence. There meets the Happy Homemakers Club to practice rituals repeated countless times every month in countless communities across rural America.

The ritual is consistent with the character of the old building in which the folk meet. The meeting is opened with a devotional reading from the Bible and includes singing two verses of *America.*

The highlight of the meeting was the presentation of a Missouri flag to the club by State Representative Ken Legan, as well as the display of the American flag given to the club earlier by Congressman Gene Taylor.

There was no doubt that in this atmosphere of devotion, patriotism, and social intercourse, that I was among people who knew who they were and were well-pleased with their heritage in the hills and hollows around Windyville.

### Jim Hamilton

## Comments on Chewin'

I remember my Grandpa Daly chewin' tobacco.

That was one of those things that old men did back then. When he needed a chaw, he'd reach into his pants pocket and pull out a hard plug of something like Pick Chewing Tobacco. From his other pocket he would pull out a pocket knife, open it up, and slice off a goodly chaw.

I was little then, and that was a long time ago, but I seem to recall a number of coffee cans around the sign shop. I always thought they were for paint brushes, but perhaps not.

As I remember Grandpa Daly, that plug of tobacco was as much a part of him as the thick, gray hair, baggy trousers, scratchy sweater, smell of turpentine, and camel hair lettering brush. Don't know why he chewed. Doubt that he did, either, and don't suppose it matters in the least. Never occured to me as a boy to ask Grandpa about his habits, or even that he had habits. Never thought of him any differently than he was. He was Grandpa Daly, period.

Whatever reason he had for chewin', I doubt it was because he thought it was the macho thing to do. Probably never even heard of the word.

Chewin' tobacco has come a long way since Grandpa's day. It's no longer reserved for old men sitting on the front stoop swapping lies about the way things used to be.

Times have changed. Tobacco chewin's not a disgusting, nasty habit to some anymore, not since the Madison Avenue crowd took it up. These days, a healthy chaw of tobacco wedged between the jawbone and

## River Of Used To Be

cheek, is about as glamorous as smoking used to be, back before the doctors started saying all those not-so-glamorous things about lung diseases.

Real men--macho men--chew.

Just look at the commercials. No old-timers pulling plugs from their pockets, just big, healthy, strapping cowboys, race car drivers, lumberjacks, longshoremen, mountain men, and athletes pulling wads of leaf tobacco, or pinches of smokeless tobacco, from brightly colored foil pouches and tins.

Couldn't be anything nasty about their habits, surely not. And the way those buxom blondes cling to them. . . .

And look at those teeth. Not a yellow one in the bunch. And never, as we are used to seeing in the old men, is there a tell-tale amber dribble from the corners of their mouths.

Fact is, if I hadn't seen them take wads of tobacco from the pouch, I'd swear these fellows didn't really chew at all.

That's how far tobacco has come. Today, it's neat!

Taking a stroll down "tobacco road" in your friendly neighborhood market, you'll come across a lot of familiar names along the way--Beech Nut, Red Man, Union, and others. But, you'll also come across a variety of tobaccos packaged to suit whatever image you have of yourself.

Now there's Big Red, with a picture of a longhorn steer across the front of it, for the cowboy fans. There is Duke for John Wayne fans. Would-be mountain men can warm up to smokeless Hawken or Kodiak, and more international sports can enjoy the old favorite, Copenhagen.

## Jim Hamilton

Engineers might like to carry a pouch of Chattanooga Chew, and hunters might like to chase a chaw of Red Fox. Miners could dig into a pouch of R.J. Gold. At pulling contests, it seems like Workhorse should be the choice, and for local magistrates, I would think the obvious selection would be the new chew, H.B. Scott.

Ever since tobacco chewin' moved in from the barn lot and onto the television screen, one small detail has bothered me: Those big strapping fellow on the commercials--don't they ever have to spit?

I guess the Madison Avenue boys never thought it out that far. Everybody I ever knew who chewed had to spit now and then. Of course, that kind of takes the edge off the glamour and causes those gals to back up a few steps. Likely they'll think twice before coaxing a kiss out of Mr. Macho after they see the leaf on his teeth.

Best I can figure, these guys are so macho they don't just chew tobacco, they eat the stuff when they're done.

Reckon I would have to admit, under those circumstances, it takes a real man to chew.

Bullfeathers, you say. Tell me, then. Did you ever see one of them riding off into the sunset with his reins in one hand and a spit cup in the other?

Pftooooooi...............splat!

## Discourse On Pleasures Of Fishing

I like fishing. I like fishing for bass, perch, crappie, goggle-eye, suckers, catfish, drum, or whatever else I can get to bite.

## River Of Used To Be

Of course, more than just fishing, I like to catch fish.

I'm not particular about what I catch them on. I'm not one of those city-bred fly rod floppers in hip boots who turns his nose up at anything that won't hit a dry fly, though I like fishing with a fly rod.

And, I'm sure not one of those bass boat boozers who thinks fishing is racing between the snags and trees on Stockton Lake in a $15,000 bass patrol boat, complete with sonar, barometer, CB, stereo, and a live well full of Coors.

I'm not convinced that bigmouth bass live on metalflake blue electric eels, or that a fishing rod has to cost $59.95.

I've never seen it proven that fishing success is measured in direct proportion to the amount of money invested.

Fishing is not a spectator sport. I don't much care for watching somebody else fish, and I sure don't like a bunch of people looking over my shoulder when I'm trying to cast.

Fishing is not a competitive sport. I don't like to fight anybody for a spot to fish.

Fishing is not a team sport. A couple of fishing buddies is plenty. More is a water circus.

Though I like dogs, fishing is seldom enhanced by the presence of a couple of hounds.

I like catching fish. Crowds, hound dogs, or any other gawking, splashing, noisy entourage is not conducive to catching fish.

Now, as for catching fish, once I've left these accoutrements of the Great American Fishing Trip behind, I'm not particular what I catch them on. Lures

## Jim Hamilton

are fine, if they work. Minnows, grasshoppers, and crawdads are usually a good bet, but for all-around fishing, I like worms.

Worms. Name me a fish you can't catch on worms and I'll not eat it. I've caught about everything there is to catch around here on worms, from bullheads to smallmouth and hog suckers to rainbow trout.

String a worm on a hook and drop it in a likely looking hole on the river and you're never sure what you're going to get, but the chances are good you will get something. That's what I like about worms. Getting something is what fishing is all about.

There are times, though, when even worms aren't good enough. They might work, but breakfast cereal works better. More about that in a minute.

I like fishing. I like catching fish, and I like catching big fish, so sometimes I like going after the biggest fish in the river--carp.

Perch, bass, crappie, and all the rest are just fine, and really good eating, but there are times when I like to test my equipment. And there's no better fish to test your tackle on than a carp.

Figure that a four pounder is a small one. Five or six pounds is about average, and to catch one on the river is not unusual.

When I was younger I used to fish for them in McDaniel Lake. About fifteen pounds was the biggest I ever caught. Took me twenty minutes or more to land it on ten-pound test line. Lucky I didn't catch one of the really big ones--thirty-five to forty pounds. There were some in there.

Back before Pomme de Terre was impounded, twelve to fourteen pound carp were common in the river

## River Of Used To Be

down around Fair Grove. We took home several.

The lake changed that; the big ones moved out and the little ones moved in by the thousands. That was back when folks were going to Nemo and catching them by the sackful on canned corn. They were about a pound each.

That wasn't carp fishing. Fortunately, today the little ones have thinnned out and there are some big ones in the river again.

Most folks don't consider carp a sport fish, probably because they don't strike a lure. But trying to land a seven or eight pounder on the river, when the fish wants to go to the brush, is about all the sport the average fisherman, even a better-than-average fisherman, can handle.

Fishing for carp starts, naturally, with a good carp hole. Find a long hole in the river with lots of cover and some shallows at one end and you've likely found a good carp hole.

If they're in there you'll see 'em. On a hot afternoon you may see these bottom-feeding monsters feeding near the surface around some bush in the water. If they are, you see their trail of muddy water boiling to the surface, or you can watch for bubbles coming to the surface in deeper water.

Rigging and baiting for carp is simple. We've tried a lot of variations, but the easiest and most effective way to catch a carp is to buy a box of Wheaties, Breakfast of Champions.

At the river, wet a handful of Wheaties, roll them into a sticky doughball, give them a couple of minutes to toughen up, and you've got a first class carp bait. Use a big hook, big enough to put a doughball on about half

# Jim Hamilton

the size of a golf ball, and don't use a sinker.

Throw it out where they should be--on the shoals where they're feeding or out a ways from their cover. Don't get it back in the brush or you'll never get him out.

Set down the pole with the bail open or the reel handle where it will turn freely, and wait. When a carp picks up a Wheaties ball, he generally makes a run with it like a freight train. He doesn't just nibble. A tight line that won't feed off the reel just about guarantees lost tackle.

Some of the big ones at the lake used to take off so hard that they would pull the rod towards the water as the line fed off. It happens fast, but you may have to wait a while for it to happen. And when he gets going, stop him. Rear back and set the hook hard. Once the carp is hooked, he'll run up and down the river and try to head for cover.

They're not easy to get in. Part of a carp's mouth is tough, but he has no bone in his lip so it's not uncommon for the hook to tear out. A hook that's too small, or an inexperienced fisherman who tries to horse him in, can mean a lost fish.

After you get him tired down, there is one thing you can almost always count on--he's not that tired! A carp almost always will make one last hard run once he gets near the bank and sees you. Be ready to give him line; he's going to take it one way or another.

Carp can be eaten, they're just kind of bony. They are far from being my favorite eating fish, but I can't think of anything that's a bigger challenge to handle once he's hooked.

The best reason for fishing for carp these days,

especially in the Pomme de Terre, is simply because that's what's there. You're kidding yourself to think that you can bring home a nice string of smallmouth bass and black perch like the good old days before the dam.

Too proud to admit you like fishing for carp should you learn you might like it? Just tell your bass boat buddy that you're making the best of a bad situation. You don't have to admit that you really like catching eight or ten pounds of fish and bringing them home in a tow sack.

Or you could ask them to join you.

I would.

## Tailgates

I've never been to a tailgate party.

From what I've heard, you can't go to a college or professional stadium event, particularly a football game, without warming up first in the parking lot with a tailgate party.

I guess that's why I've never been to a tailgate party. I don't go to football games, other than local ones, and nobody seems to be partying much before or after those thrashings. Must be some school rule against it.

I've been to only one college football game, and that was twenty-five years ago at a Southwest Missouri State College homecoming game. I didn't see much in Coach Red Cross's Bears to make me want to watch another. And I don't think tailgate parties had been invented yet.

Though I've never been to one of today's fabled tailgate parties, I am not, however, unfamiliar with

# Jim Hamilton

tailgates.

As a matter of fact, I can't imagine owning a pickup truck without one. That horizontal slab of sheet metal hinged to the end of the pick-up box is the most versatile and useful part of the truck, the best thing to happen to motorized transportation since running boards which were also, may they rest in peace, pretty darned useful.

The best tailgates were found on pick-ups made in the forties and fifties, maybe in the sixties. They were single, flat sheets of heavy sheet metal. Instead of having locks like doors, they fastened up or down with hooks on the end of a chain and could be adjusted to hang at an angle or be dropped down against the bumper clean out of the way. Best of all, you never had trouble finding a flat spot to set a cup of coffee. Or yourself.

These days, the hollow, beer can-thin sheet metal gates are still handier than trying to find a flat rock in the woods, but some of them have some serious utility shortcomings. There is hardly a flat spot on them! Little ridges and depressions make the flimsy sheet metal sturdier, but they don't offer much comfort for the posterior, and it is nearly impossible to set down a coffee cup or soda pop can without seeing it spill.

I solved that shortcoming on my Chevy by bolting a slab of plywood to the inside of the tailgate. Can't imagine why some genius in Detroit hasn't already figured it out and offered a two dollar tailgate flattener as a $500 option.

I'm sure there are enough tailgate partiers in Detroit that one should have figured out that a tailgate does much more than enclose the pick-up box: It makes

# River Of Used To Be

a great table for weiner roasts and picnics, and is indispensible as a kitchen counter when you're living out of a camper shell.

## Sidewalks and Proches

Politicans have lots of ideas about what is wrong with this country, but I've not heard one of them mention two of the most obvious: The demise of sidewalks and the decline of front porches.

We don't build enough sidewalks. I don't know when we stopped, but we did. In Grandpa's day we wouldn't have built a city street without putting a walk on either side of it.

Today, it is exceptional to see a sidewalk built on even one side of the street. Of all the housing developments to sprawl around our towns during the past half-century or so, few have included sidewalks.

If you want to use a sidewalk, you have to walk in the old part of town. Modern folks, it seems, have no need for them. The few sidewalks we have are mostly crumbling, broken, and turned askew in earthquake fashion by roots and sinking soil.

Walking in newer parts of town is not encouraged unless you like to share the street with passing cars. Overgrown and often narrow highway shoulders plunging into ditches make walking along state roads even more precarious.

Why did we quit building sidewalks? Did folks stop walking because it was easier to drive? The automobile, I am sure, had something to do with it.

We are all equal on sidewalks. The automobile

## Jim Hamilton

made us something different, or something more. It didn't just transport, it transformed us. Moreover, it isolated us in two tons of steel.

When we used sidewalks we were vulnerable, more equal, more ourselves. Folks passing on a sidewalk looked one another in the eye, generally had to smile, and even offer a greeting. It was hard not to know your neighbors when you all used sidewalks. Young men enjoyed bashful, blushing encounters with finely dressed young ladies on Sunday morning. Neighborhoods came together on sidewalks--kids on tricycles and scooters, neigbors walking to the corner store.

Front porches faced the sidewalks and tree-lined streets, and here and there folks relaxed in rocking chairs or squeaked in porch swings.

Front porches were built to catch cool breezes on summer evenings, or provide respite from the midday sun. They were a grandstand from which to watch the neighborhood pass by, to sip tea or coffee, and watch kids chase fireflies or play with their trikes on the sidewalk.

Front porches are friendly--an invitation for passersby to stop and visit or simply shout greetings from the sidewalk.

Front porches disappeared about the same time as sidewalks. That's understandable--they went together.

Front porches were replaced by backyard patios and decks, places where entire families could sequester themselves behind privacy fences and ranch style homes.

Out front, where the porch used to be, was built a little step, and a puny gable hung over the door. Seldom used, the front door was locked and the front yard as sterile as astroturf. The family came in through the garage, seldom having to face the neighborhood except through the tinted glass of their automobiles.

Sidewalks and front porches. There are still a few around, but too few. Automobiles, air conditioning, and television are all to blame, I suppose. With all these modern things, sidewalks and front porches have become antiques.

Perhaps we gave them up too soon, our friendly sidewalks and front porches. Maybe we turned our backs on the places where our neighbors were nurtured and lost the time we once took to enjoy them.

## He Knew Cars

A flag was raised at Fair Grove Saturday evening. The brass plate on the base honored several from the community who could not be on hand for the simple ceremony.

Among those named were three generations of the Lucas family--Glen, Jack, and Don. They were among us, but unseen.

Don was a classmate of mine at Fair Grove High, another graduate of the Class of 1965. He was laid to rest this Father's Day, just forty-five years old when he died June 18.

I hadn't seen "Luke" much since high school, yet he was as familiar around Fair Grove as the old mill across from his late father's garage.

Those times I ran into him at the annual reunions and ice cream socials, or on my regular newspaper business visits to town, he was always the same: Tall and smiling a broad grin in his trademark bib overalls. It was

## Jim Hamilton

rare to see him otherwise dressed. I don't recall what he wore to our twenty-fifth anniversary alumni banquet, but it was not his overalls.

Even after cancer had claimed a leg, Don's affable spirit and good-natured grin seemed hardly dimmed. He could still ride his cycle and life was still good.

Luke was still very much the guy we knew in high school--a good student and athlete--but, more importantly, a gifted mechanic. He had a special quality the rest of us respected and envied: He understood the automobile.

Born into a family of mechanics, Luke must have had a grease pit for a playpen and a torque wrench for a pacifier.

In high school he drove a black primer-painted '41 Chevy coupe he kept humming like a sewing machine. Once, after high school, I recall watching him adjust the lifters on a Ford V-8. The engine looked like one of those plastic classroom models, clean as a watch, opaque streams of oil pumping as clear as when it first came from the can.

There was, if not magic, at least some mysticism in his understanding of automobiles.

I would not condense a man's life to memories of a surgically clean Ford V-8, translucent streams of thirty-weight oil, and the broad grin of a lanky mechanic in bib overalls leaning over a '56 Ford fender, but those are images I most vividly recall. As a husband and father, I know Don Lucas was much more, but I would offer with deep regard and great respect this simple praise:

He knew cars.

# River Of Used To Be

## Accident Victim

I have just returned from the scene of an auto accident which took the life of a well-known Buffalo teenager, a member of a prominent family, a popular, attractive young lady, somewhat of a celebrity as a high school softball pitcher.

I've been writing about auto accidents for years. I've seen several, have covered dozens of them.

You would think a reporter would become calloused and insensitive to the tragedy. Most don't, and I don't think I ever will.

In the past two nights I have been to two serious auto accidents near Buffalo. I felt a wrenching emptiness as I came upon the wreckage of the first and heard who was involved. I know them, too. By some miracle the mother and two daughters survived. Not so at the accident tonight.

Nights like these try to rob a reporter of his objectivity. It becomes more difficult when he must record unpleasant news, the tragedies of real people. Not just names from a report or a telephone book, but people he knows.

That, perhaps, is one of the toughest parts of journalism in a small community. Every tragedy hits close to home. When the ambulance goes out, there is always the fear of finding a friend, neighbor, or relative at the other end.

Journalism textbooks preach objectivity, and experience and training reinforces it. But it really isn't that easy. The words may be objective, but behind them is another real person.

Standing in the glow of flashing red lights, looking

## Jim Hamilton

at the wreckage, listening to the police car radio blare, and listing the names of victims, there is no escaping the anguish of human tragedy, not even for we who must simply report it.

# Part Four

# WINTERFALL TO FROST

## Images Of The Seasons

# Winterfall

Winter fell on us Sunday like a chill wind through a sweaty T-shirt.

The day broke with a soft drizzle tapping on crisp leaves and wallowed through the hours mixing a dreary muck, slogging into bone-chilling night. It was a hot chocolate evening for playing old records, reading novels and toasting feet through well-worn socks while oak flames danced on the Isinglass in the cast iron door of our old woodstove.

Birdshot pellets rattled lightly in the hours before light. Monday morning found car tops iced with a crunchy white frosting and random snowflakes drifting like lost feathers after a pillow fight.

November arrived on such a warm wind but we should not have been deceived. Short-lived autumn brilliance dimmed as trees shed their leaves, stark skeletons of elm and walnut looking more prepared than we for the north wind's blustery spitting and freezing sprees.

Though by written record winter is more than a month away, the look of autumn's browning hills tells a tale more true. Narrow days and growing breadth of night bespeak of winterfall. As Tuesday's light frost stuck to windshields like a new coat of paint, expect this visitor to stay a spell.

Though days and nights such as these in other months may seem fair, a welcome respite from the mercury's plunge, they now seem cold to these warm-weather bones. So, bank the fire before you retire and tuck the covers under you tight. Heed November's warnings of cold winter nights.

### Jim Hamilton

## Winter Courting

The cold, damp breath of winter courted Monday, waking us sharply from the langour of long, dry October days and balmy nights with bedroom windows raised to catch southern breezes.

Visiting on November winds and high, gray clouds piled on the horizon, winter awakened us to savor the chatter of chainsaws and the sap-sweet aroma of oak sawdust piling at our feet.

Gently she called this season, biding her time until the full fall symphony of colors had been played in the woodland ridges and glades. Reluctant, she was, to turn brown the pallete of russet red and sunlight yellows, slow to make the trees' limbs quiver, their robes to drop at their feet.

By the stargazers' charts, she should wait a while more. December 22 is the calendar-maker's date for her arrival. Yet, she visits now, if not planning to stay, painting dun landscapes with skeleton trees on sagegrass hills.

Welcome is this November coming, as is that December day when she comes the season to stay. Welcome the bite on our ears, and the glistening blanket of silver flecked with fire and gold by the morning sunrise.

Winter, though a bleak and icy bride, we embrace to temper our souls with hardship uncommon to summer, to refresh our spirits with strengths and resolve.

Winter's dowry is that season of carrying in wood and feeding fires late at night, of rising early to chop ice on the pond, of feeding dogs in the snow and fixing fences with fingers icy cold, that season when jobs simple

# River Of Used To Be

in any other season become taxing chores, a hard season of scarce money, and work that profits little but survival.

Winter brings, too, that warming season of woodsmoke and wet wool smells, of britches legs toasting behind the stove. Ears are warmed by the baying of hounds on the trail of a cottontail, heads filed with the smell of new leather gloves, and of gun oil.

We're children again, shuffling through the woods half to our knees in leaves. Alfalfa hay bales are broken open in the feed bunk. Snow melts on the cow's backs and calves are safely in the barn. Hot chocolate steams in the kitchen, popcorn warms the evening, and on quiet nights snow falls like a white quilt while as we lay warm under quilts of our own.

Winter comes courting on these first days of November. Welcome is her season of woodsmoke and holidays.

## Every Snow Should So Softly Fall

Every snow should come and go as did last Saturday's.

It was everything a snowfall should be and none of those nasty things snow often is but we wish it weren't.

It was a White Christmas kind of black-and-white TV movie snow--huge, fluffy flakes drifting down before dawn in blue mecury lights. A rumpled white blanket lay on the ground. Brown flowers in the planter out front were flocked, and the cedars in the fencerow robed in fleece.

The air was warm, barely freezing by first light as

## Jim Hamilton

the goosedown flakes kept fluttering around and down, as in the last round of a pillow fight, settling in piles on the gatepost, barbed-wire fence, and chrome pick-up wheel rims.

Along the roadside, sparrows flitted and redbirds fluttered back and forth across the road just ahead of my steps which dusted snow from the old ragweed tops and sheltering scrubby oaks.

But for the wingbeats of birds the air was still, hushed by the cottony muff.

Yes, Saturday's snow was everything a snow should be, draping the morning in an ermine robe, just wet and deep enough to spawn snowball fights, or make a snowman grow from balls rolled in twisting, green tracks around the yard.

No need for four-wheel-drives to get to work, or snowplow trucks with their flashing yellow lights. It wasn't that kind of snow--more like melt-in-your-mouth, fluffy frosting on an angel food cake.

Well before dinner it had stopped, leaving three or four inches piled on the truck.

I spent the afternoon in Springfield where little real snow fell, but just the smell of the stuff brought at least a half-million people out to Christmas shop. Before dark we were safely out of that crowd and home, and the perfect snow was gone.

Every snow should so gently come and go.

## Camp Of The Frozen Coffee Pot

Maybe it was the yapping howl of coyotes on a distant ridge. Camp called us back down the frosty river

## River Of Used To Be

bottom.

In the dark canyon below our trail the roar of water rushing across polished stone drew us cautiously toward the edge of rock ledges where we shined our flashlights on the boiling water. The river wasn't as big as it sounded, or the canyoned walls of the shut-in rapids so tall as they seemed when only darkness lay over the brink. On the ridge high above the river, along what we surmised to be the Ozark Trail, a faint yellow light and wisp of smoke betrayed a solitary backpacker.

Holding to the trail, we turned our lights off so we could be guided by the light of the moon just climbing over the ridge. Camp still called us back to the smoldering fire, back to our tents and sleeping bags where we would cocoon ourselves against the bite of a bitter January night.

We had known, Steve and I, as we packed for this weekend at Johnson Shut-Ins, that it would not be a trip for faint spirits. Back at the office the ladies all thought us crazy. Our wives and kids agreed.

But, what did they know, these women and children, of the primal instincts which drive men to the wilderness.

We would not be denied our escape. We went prepared to meet the cold head-on. My old Stihl chain saw took little space in the back of the truck, and ample deadfall in the nearby national forest provided wood for a blazing fire.

Earlier in the evening we had crowded close to the flames, roasting skewered cubes of beef over the coals, drinking strong coffee, and agreeing that our women and children would never have appreciated the rigors of eating dinner in insulated gloves. Bundled

## Jim Hamilton

against the rising wind in long johns, overalls, parkas, stocking caps, and every other stitch of clothing we could find, we cussed our jobs, our bosses, our wives, and the overall gentility of civilized society. We heartily declared it a great camp, and every time we stood to toast our frozen backsides, we remarked on the pristine quiet and beauty of the starlit night and regretted that we had not brought our pipes and cigars.

The late-night walk down to the shut-ins took us past the only other campers in the park. We had heard their voices and through the trees caught a glimpse of their campfire nearly a quarter of a mile away. We hollered howdy from the shadowy trail, and their talking suddenly stopped as the three men looked up from their campfire and tried to make us out.

"Man, you gave us a scare," said one bulky fellow in a stocking cap. "We thought we were the only ones crazy enough to be camped out here tonight." We assured them that they weren't, noting that their pickup camper looked a lot warmer than our tents.

We visited for a few minutes. One of the campers was from Columbia, the other from Joplin, another from St. Louis. The guy with the camper had done a lot of driving to pick the others up, because the shut-ins were nowhere close to any of their homes. As we left, they were passing around a bottle of what one claimed to be Irish whiskey, filling the air with cigar smoke, and having a boisterously great time which their wives and children would not have appreciated.

The walk to the river gave us a unique perception of the shut-ins, a natural wonder with grandeur heard like the rising roar of applause at our arrival. Our dim flashlights could scarcely reveal the source of that

## River Of Used To Be

nocturnal roar. We would see the rocks and rushing water in the early morning sun.

Back at camp we felt warmed by the brisk walk, and elected to turn in before the comfort turned to a chill. Steve suggested we fill the coffee pot before crawling into our tents.

Moonlight sparkled on the frost as we kicked the ends of sticks into the coals and banked the fire with a couple of half-green oak logs as big around as pie plates.

The tents and sleeping bags fended off the cold well enough, except for those too-frequent excursions when I had to crawl out of that heap of coats and covers, unzip the frosty tent fly, and tiptoe downhill for a few seconds of relief.

Five or six degrees, we figured. I had stripped to my long johns, piled extra blankets on my sleeping bag, and slept with a stocking cap over my ears.

But winter gear couldn't insulate us from the racket of campers who pulled in around midnight in a Datsun with a raspy front wheel-bearing. Of ninety-eight open camping spots, they picked one fifty yards away and slept in the car, starting the engine now and then to get warm.

I wondered if they would have coffee in the morning. I hoped they wouldn't. I hoped they would drop by and ask for a cup. I wanted to boot them back to St. Louis, especially the cute one with the long blond hair and gold earring who came whizzing by our campsite at daybreak on rollerblades looking for the bathroom.

Come morning, every drop of water in camp was frozen solid, including two five-gallon cubes. Our potatoes were as hard as the polished rocks on a Black

# Jim Hamilton

River gravel bar. Our cans of soda had blown up, popping their tops with a report that sounded like a .22 rifle.

But we soon had coffee. I tossed kindling and dry pine logs on the smoldering coals. A half-hour later and the frozen coffee pot was thawed and perking.

It took us a little longer.

Thawed by a breakfast of fried potatoes and sausage, and encouraged by the clear sky and fire-orange rim on the ridge, we walked back to the shut-ins and hiked the two and one-half mile trail, the omnipresent roar of the Black River rushing over granite boulders growing to a deafening din as we approached the polished chutes.

High on the gray ridge we saw a flash of color, the backpacker's tent draped over some brush to dry. We wondered aloud what kind of night he'd had.

We were led along the trail by a yellow dog we called Phantom. She was an old yeller kind of half-hound with the instincts of Lassie leading us to Timmy. She met us at the onset of our hike, guided us across the rocky ledges, down to the river's edge, and back up narrow old logging roads rutted with the footsteps of countless others who had preceded us.

When we digressed to scout a gravel bar, or left the trail to take pictures of a frozen waterfall, Phantom waited patiently for us to return to the marked path. We later made half the hike again to recover a lost glove. Phantom, who had lost nothing, did not go. We never saw her again.

Saturday warmed rapidly, and on a two-hour climb up Bell Mountain, so did we. The trail, at times, was just a trace across rocky barrens and stands of

## River Of Used To Be

hardwood, leading us to surmise that we were two of but a few modern Natty Bumpos who would undertake to find this trail to the top. Then the trace widened into an old road, and at more than 1,700 feet we found a U.S. Geological Service marker and the foundations of an old fire lookout tower. Others had been here before, but not recently.

The summit offered a spectacular view, where from atop an outcropping of rock we declared the vista of surrounding mountains and Shut-Ins Creek worth the climb and were immensely satisfied with ourselves for accomplishing it. We wished we had brought our pipes.

On the trail down and at least two miles up the mountain, we met a fellow with his eight-year-old daughter skipping along behind him, her purple Nikes bouncing from rock to rock as they crossed a grassy seep. He was carrying a bow, said he might take a shot at a rabbit. They had been on the mountain for hours looking for shed deer antlers. Her only prize was a turkey feather.

We learned that earlier she and her dad had become seperated as she lingered on the trail. Lost and alone in the woods for nearly an hour, she told us she almost cried. Almost? We reckoned either one of us would have.

They, too, were on their way down. We scurried to get ahead of them, not wishing to be slowed by a child on the trail. An hour later, our trip shortened by a dead-reckoning cut-off, we arrived at the parking lot sore and exhausted. A blister was throbbing, and I wished I had shed my heavy long johns. But we had challeneged Bell mountain, climbed her to the top, beheld her beauty, and returned to tell others of it. It was the kind of climb boys make to prove their virility and old men recall with a glimmer in their eye.

Yes, we had earned a cold soda. As we lifted the frosty cans to our lips, we heard the bubbly voice of the little girl we had met on the trail: "Race you to the truck, Daddy." Ah, youth.

Saturday night was warmer and we slept soundly. Fatigue subdued the noise that tents and sleeping bags could not insulate. The water only froze some, not solid.

We broke camp early Sunday. Our noisy neighbors had the front wheel off their Datsun and looked to be homesteading.

We had no reason to stay. All challenges after Friday night had been timid ones, even the climb up Bell Mountain, compared to the morning of the frozen coffee pot.

It was a camping trip worth telling about and, most importantly, one worth improving upon with every telling.

## Signs of Spring

Old Man Winter may have a few nasty surprises waiting in the wings, but these sunny days make it feel awfully near spring.

By the calendar, March 20, the first day of spring, is yet a month away. But even now, we begin to see some early signs that the new season is just around the corner:

* Bugs on the bumper.
* Ticks in our britches.

## River Of Used To Be

* Dead worms on the driveway after a rain.
* Slugs on the sidewalk.
* Kid's coats left at school.
* Garlic in the milk.
* Runny noses.
* Six sticks of firewood left, and the field is too wet to go get more.
* Propane gas tank on ten percent, and it better last.
* Income tax forms still piled on the kitchen table.
* Calves.
* Freshly oiled fishing reels dripping on the rug in the corner of the family room.
* Dust on the shotgun.
* Grass growing in the back of the pickup truck.
* Wasps in the outhouse.
* Snakes in the grass.
* Turtles in the road.
* Itching and scratching.
* Joggers in shorts.
* Green wood too sappy to burn.
* Elm buds.
* Sassafrass tea.
* Freshly cooked maple syrup.
* Fresh haircuts.
* Johnny Jump-ups.
* Brighter dispositions.
* Garden seed racks in the store.
* Empty hayloft.
* Bank account to match the hayloft.
* Local political campaigns.
* Frivolous newspaper columns.

# Jim Hamilton

## Battle For The Bean Patch

I have seen the enemy and he is not us.

He's a whistle pig. A groundhog. Maybe the entire clan,

Our battlefield is a sorry-looking swatch of sloping soil I call my garden, a rock-riddled pile of fill and fertilizer, salted with broken beer bottles and old carburetor parts.

An adequate bean and tomato patch, it is to generations of groundhogs a sacred place, hallowed soil soaked with the blood of their brothers.

It is also the source of tender sweet pea salads, blushing pink tomato desserts, and savory sweet corn nibblings.

One season I grew green beans, roastin' ears, and more tomatoes than we could eat. Word got around. Next year the groundhogs beat us to the harvest.

Rows of lettuce were neatly shorn and green beans and peas nipped to the ground. Entire sections of the garden just disappeared overnight. One evening I watered the beans and reported, "We'll have a mess to eat by Saturday." Come morning they were gone.

Vanished!

Last year I gave in. I grew only potatoes, radishes, and onions. Funny how something called a groundhog won't dig for dinner. Or, maybe they don't care for spuds, onions, and radishes. They made short work of my vain attempt to grow leaf lettuce. We had one mess. They had breakfast for a month. That was last year.

The robins are back. Gardening time is near. I'll not back down again.

Groundhogs beware. Land mines are illegal;

# River Of Used To Be

besides, too many kids and dogs running loose. Shooting works, but it ain't that easy. They are sneaky varmints, and always die with a belly full of my best tomatoes.

Looks like the best offense may be a good defense, or just a fence. Woven wire.

I'm gonna fence 'em out. Let 'em eat steel!

I hope to grow the plumpest, juciest red tomatoes ever, just across that fence. I want ol' whistle pig to see what he won't get to taste. I'll drive him crazy, just like he's done to me for the last five years.

It'll cost a few bucks, and my wife and kids think I'm the one who's crazy. We could buy a lot of vegetables for the price of a roll of wire.

Vegetables!

This has nothing to do with vegetables.

The glove has been dropped. It's war.

No lousy groundhog is going to stop me from growing green beans in my own backyard, no matter what it costs.

Even if it grows nothing but weeds, I will have my garden this year, and my furry foes will have to learn to live on what I throw over the fence.

And the kids are gonna have to learn to really like green beans.

## Tales Told In The Face Of An Axe

I marvel each spring at the life which emerges from the decaying floor of my woods.

Cowslip and violet, and countless tiny flowers, the names of which I've never known, push aside the musty leaves and sprinkle the floor with color. Between green

## Jim Hamilton

clumps of garlic, forests of mayapples unfold like umbrellas.

Dogwood blossoms are about to turn, while serviceberry flocks twisted limbs in saintly white.

Kicking through the leaves on a warm April evening, I expect to see a black snake slithering through the leaves where I'd seen it once before, when something catches my eye, something foreign beneath the rounded contours of rotting leaves with a few sprigs of green around it, a hard line.

I step closer and kick the leaves aside. It's darker than the leaves, though about the same mottled brown. I lift it from its bed, leaving its impression in the damp leaves. It's hard, wet, cold in my hand--an old axe head. Well-used and filed down to a portion of its original size, the old double-bitted head might have been thrown away.

Not likely, though. More likely it was lost, misplaced, left leaning against a tree, or knocked over by a hound, and forgotten. I hold it in my hand and read its story.

It had lain silent for years. Seasons of rain, snow, and piling leaves have left their scars--deep rusted pits--on either side of its face, though the blade still holds an edge.

Where an oak handle had once been driven tightly into the head, black humus fills the hole. The woods has reclaimed its own.

Countless handles have held the old axe head. Heavy hammer marks dent the base where it's been pounded off old handles, or maybe driven free from a block of wood too tight to split.

It was no woodsman's tool. It was a hard-working

## River Of Used To Be

farmer's axe, used to clear brush as well as top limbs from trees. It tells the same story as my grandad's axe, my dad's axe, the axe I used as a boy, and the one I use now.

Some years ago a farmer took this old axe, swung it over his shoulder, and buried the dull side in a stump. Taking a file or stone from his overalls pocket, he honed the edge to razor sharpness.

Then, with the razor edge, he severed branches the size of his wrist from a tree felled earlier with a crosscut. Swung powerfully from the right and the left, the axe bit saucer-sized chunks from the log, sending them flying into the brush.

Then, with the same axe, buckbrush and gooseberry were grubbed out of the ground as the head sent dirt and amber sparks flying.

The same axe, just like my axe, one side kept like a skinner's knife, the other more like a grubbing hoe. It might have been mine. But, it wasn't. It was part of another's life.

An axe is more than a tool. A man gets attached to an axe. Even if he has two or three, one is the favorite.

I imagine the fellow who misplaced this axe was a spell getting used to the loss. The new one he bought at the hardware store didn't have the same feel. It took a while before he could hit the center of a log. He hit the dirt a lot. It didn't feel quite right, kind of like a borrowed axe.

He probably made a trip or two back to the woods where he thought he last leaned it. but maybe it was lost under leaves, or under snow. He came back luckless, a guilty bluetick hound at his feet.

## Jim Hamilton

I've got no idea who last swung this axe. I can't guess how many years it lay hidden beneath the leaves.

But, from the lines of age and wear in the old axe head, I know something about the one who used it. Doubtlessly separated by generations, we've something in common.

I can feel it as I hold the rusty old head and run my fingers along the sharp edge, while the blunted, dull blade rests comfortably in my palm.

Now, if I should lose my axe, years from now I hope someone might pick it up and wonder whose it was. If he is in what is now my woods, he might marvel that some old-timer years ago sharpened the axe just as he does, and he'll feel a kinship that bridges years and generations, a kinsmanship that bonds all men who have ever set out for the woods with old axes resting on their shoulders.

He'll hold the rusty head in his hand and imagine me in overalls, kneeling over an axe like his, the tang of a mill bastard file in the heel of my right hand, silvery filings falling to the dark stump with every stroke I take.

## Life's The Berries

May.

It's that season of sultry evenings and cool mornings when spring ambles toward summer, crushing the cheat and hopclover with every step.

Redbud trees are now green. Dogwood blossoms have fluttered into obscurity. The sweet fragrance of the lilac bush has faded. Yards beg for mowing every weekend, and gardens sprout morning glory vines.

## River Of Used To Be

Down in the low meadow, in little-grazed patches of pasture, hiding under the shade of towering ten-inch grass and weeds, the terrapin's orchard begins to bear its succulent, scarlet fruit.

Strawberries. Wild strawberries.

Just this Mother's Day I tasted the season's first tiny, sweet bites, the forerunners of more to follow with longer days, a little rain, and warmer nights.

Where now no random scarlet berries hang hiding under umbrellas of palm-like leaves, the meadow will shortly scream with pinpoints of red. Terrapins, likely, will reap the harvest.

But, that was not so likely in a generation past. I recall as a boy the adventure and joy of discovering new, lush patches of untouched wild strawberries, where my brothers and I fell to our knees and joined the terrapins in a veritable feast of the juicy, tiny fruit. Hours we spent, and never ate our fill.

But wild strawberries and their telltale, crimson, Emmett Kelly grin were but a foreshadowing of the true springtime delight that lifted us from our knees to the trees.

Mulberries. Our farm was blessed with several fruitful mulberry trees. The oldest was a many-trunked octogenarian down by the old dump, but it was not our favorite.

Another I recall was a little tree in the edge of the woods with late, plump, shiny berries, but it was too small when I was just the right size.

*The* mulberry tree was a stout-limbed sanctuary that grew just across the barnlot near the corner of the woods.

To my brother, Russell, and me, that was the

# Jim Hamilton

most hospitable tree. We climbed her as easily as our grandmother's kitchen steps, and she embraced us with arms as secure and warm as a mother's hug. Come to supper, she seemed to say, and we surely did.

Hidden in her leafy alcoves we crawled for hours to the extremities of every limb. Like 'possums, we hung by our toenails and tails to reach every last plump, juicy berry. Cradled in her sturdy arms, we nursed at Mother Nature's breast. No pleasure since has embraced me more securely than that of the mulberry tree.

Now, the old tree is long gone, fallen away with the years just like the big sassafrass that ruled the barnlot hill, and the towering oak with the grapevines we climbed like Jack's beanstalk to the giant's castle in the clouds.

But, in these waning days of May, fields still bear tiny, sweet, wild strawberries, and the little mulberry in the woods is bigger now, spreading heavy limbs, another generation to embrace.

## Dandelions

Dandelions don't get much respect; folks just don't appreciate them.

I overheard two lawn manicurists swapping terrifying tales of their war against the aggressive yellow peril, the invading weed which threatened the virtues of their unspoiled lawns.

Amusing, I thought. Such heroics just to stem the invasion of a harmless, even edible, little yellow flower.

I like dandelions. They speckle my yard like spots on a good bluetick pup, or paint on an artist's thumb.

No blight, they accentuate the greenery with their brilliant bursts of yellow. Their fuzzy balloon seedheads are a child's delight to pick, hold by the stem, and blow to speedy proliferation.

We go to great extents and expense tilling, sowing, and nurturing flowers of more dubious descent, no more beauty, and much less reliability than the scorned, but comely, dandelion.

We fight and kill the yellow squatters just to grow some spongy mass of imported grass. Now, I wonder which is *really* the weed.

A perfect yard is a boring tapestry without yellow stitches of dandelions.

When the fields and woods are full of wildflowers heralding the return of spring, let's not overlook the lowly dandelion.

Like those irreverent yellow trespassers, some folks I know are wildflowers too, adding color and zest to monotonous surroundings, unappreciated by those who want the world uniform and wrapped in plastic.

Wildflowers. Like those rapscallion dandelions, popping up here and there, invited or not, add color wherever they put down roots, turning life's drab canvas into vibrant Van Goghs.

## Images Of Summer

No season compares with summer, when the bare limbs and dun fields of December are yet easily remembered, recalled even more bleak in contrast to the verdant, deep-pile carpets of June's fields and July's jungled hollows and river bottoms. It is the season when

# Jim Hamilton

nature paints her images of summer:

* Sunflowers ten feet tall in my garden, stout volunteers from last summer's spawn, black faces encircled in mustard-colored yellow bonnets tied tightly at the chin, turned toward the morning sun.
* Broad-leaved, burgundy cannas block the back window, delicate florets roof-line tall, wisps of scarlet velvet waving from spires above the foliate wall.
* Along vines overtaking the porch and yard, yellow trumpet blossoms of winter squash greet the morning sun bejeweled in dew, only to wilt by noon and rest in the clutch of flannelled leaves.
* Careless spashes of the artist's roadside tunic, orange butterfly milkweed and trumpet vines around clusters of lavender horsemint, black-eyed susans flecked on fields like spilled glitter across rumpled lace-trimmed sheets.
* Cattails stand like green swords thrust handle-down in the bog, seedheads pierced like sausages on upturned rapier's tips.

Images of summer, extraordinary perceptions of the ordinary if we just turn our heads to see.

## Hot And Dry

It's hot and dry.
Some folks are calling it a drought. I don't know

# River Of Used To Be

if it is or not but it is the first time I ever had trouble growing cucumbers.

I was up at the lake the other day when a couple of fellows came into the marina all grimy and hot. They had been out trolling, but they said it was no use: Their boat kicked up such a cloud of dust no fish would come near.

They swore they saw shad leaving the school on account of no air conditioning, and the white bass are starting to make their run on roller skates.

Trotliners were having a time with crabgrass growing all over their line. They have to be extra careful about handling the few catfish they catch: Cockleburs in the cats' whiskers cause a nasty cut.

River men claim the water is so low a crawdad can't find a wet rock to crawl under. The only thing that seems to be thriving is the carp, but they don't need but a hatful of muddy water. They have been stretched out on gravel bars working on their tans, rubbing their scales with Coppertone pilfered from float-trippers they've dumped.

Everything along the river is suffering, even the vegetarians. Down at the springhole where the watercress grows, a gal reached in there to yank out a handful and came up with a fistful of prickly pear cactus!

Let me tell you: It's dry.


## Cool Water

Thunder shook the windows and lightning streaked across the TV screen. Welcome sounds and sights not heard or seen here for too many days.

# Jim Hamilton

Earlier in the evening we were soaked and chilled by a sudden downpour at the Little League fields. Falling on shoulders baked day-after-100-degree-day at the fair, giant drops sizzled like spit on a wood stove.

Powdery dust turned to an inch of mud, caking in gummy layers and adhering to dry shoe soles.

Sounds awful. It was great. But, it didn't last. Before I was home and into dry clothes, the rain stopped. Thunder rolled and lightning flashed, but it was just for show.

We're used to getting rain in the Ozarks, forty-four inches per year. Two weeks without a drop and we start hearing whispers of drought. It doesn't take long to dry out the shallow soil on our rocky hillsides.

It seems we get near a drought every year, and it seems to always come as a big surprise.

Every good rain rinses our memories clean. When grass is tall and ponds are full, we forget there are times when it doesn't rain. But if we will honestly recollect, just as sure as most years won't bring a prolonged drought, some years will. And even the wet years have dry weeks. Had a fellow say to me once, "Ever notice how we seem to get a big rain at the end of a drought?"

We kind of take it for granted that sooner or later it will rain. We take other water for granted, too.

The Ozarks are blessed with abundant groundwater, most of it pure and clean. We have countless lakes, streams, and ponds. Water is all around us.

Drought, we realize, can claim our farm ponds, drop our lakes to stagnant pools, and reduce our streams to trickles.

Even then, when we turn the tap we expect an

endless flow of cold water from deep within the earth, all we want or need.

Maybe we expect too much.

## Tugs Of Instinct

I've heard it theorized that folks, like dogs, come in different breeds, some of value, some not.

Though we are mostly now a mongrel horde, somewhere back in our pedigrees we can find the specialties of our genes.

No matter where we're found at work in today's world of chrome and styrofoam, we're shaken now and then by the ancestral tugs of instincts long buried by the domestication of our breed.

Now, in these Ozark hills I suspect there's many an English Appalachian breed with roots in the English woods, Irish hills, and Europe's blackest forests.

At times it seems we're more akin to a possum, coyote, bluetick hound, or blackjack tree than to others of the species with which we normally run.

First frost provides its clues, primal instincts rising in our veins. Come shorter days and cold moonlit nights, we start to sprout longer whiskers, change our colors, and go skulking through the woods in search of winter dens.

We begin to wonder how long 'til persimmons ripen, and remember days spent high in oak trees, savoring summer and possum grapes, favoring the former.

Fall is for football, entertainment for folks of a somewhat different breed. Town dogs, no matter where

## Jim Hamilton

they live.

First frost, and bluegrass lies like an early-season pelt under naked, knobby walnut trees, and the very breeze sends pungent green walnuts thumping to the sod.

Creeping vines turn red. Yellowing leaves rattle to the ground as the wind swings to the north.

You can smell the season change like overripe paw-paws scattered on the ground.

It may leave other dogs sleeping in their houses.

But, as for this Ozarks breed, we feel it jerk us to the ends of our chains.

## First Frost

I was drawn into dormancy during steamy, sweating, sultry, summer days. But frosty mornings broke the spell. Early, curly leaves are strewn across my yard on purplish crabgrass tops.

Now in my woods, acorns litter the floor, a few hidden beneath a scant scattering of scuttled leaves.

In the trees, whiskey-bottle amber hues tarnish the leaves. Sumac leaves, like pokeberry juice, stain the fence-row red.

The wind, shifting to the north, has a bite in its breath. Across a hollow or two, someone else's chain saw chuck-chucks.

Now, sitting on last year's stump--a tree I cut in knee-deep snow--I hear a whisper. No one there. . . just the woods.

A temptress blowing in my ear, the comfort of Grandma's apron, the knowing glint of steel-shot eyes beneath a father's weathered brow.

This place, or somewhere much the same, is where my soul was born, whispers the woods.

I can't, for any reason ever given me, comprehend that there's anywhere else this time of year where a man might rather be.

## Splashy October

No season compares with fall, no month with October.

The hardwood trees of the Ozarks are transformed from a monochrome of green in spring and summer to a splashy spectrum of color under October's shorter days.

Fields of prairie grasses are bejeweled by early morning frost, then rust under the October sun.

Where bluestem stands turn to purple-tinged amber seas, the bearded seeds drift like mayflies across the lapping waves emblazoned by sunlight.

On the ridges, burnished oaks are left with splashes of green, and yellow hickories burn like campfires at dawn. Along a draw, crimson sumac and ivy blaze at the foot of golden sassafrass. Up a naked walnut trunk crawls a scarlet vine, while maples burn across a distant hollow.

With all this fire and visual fury, these Ozark hills could be the victim of Van Gogh's palette, dropped in a moment of rage and the brilliant oils splattered in wild confusion.

Quietly, fall settles on the river. The path I walked easily in spring is overgrown with weeds that rustle and shatter on my shoulders, and burrs and all sorts of stickerish things cling to my trousers.

At water's edge, sycamore leaves lilt to the surface, settling lightly, to be driven across like imperiled sailing ships, piling on the windward shore. Beneath the surface, their bodies roll in the current, to disappear in the dingy depths of a glassy eddy.

## Winter Blows Petals From Marigolds

Fall is one of my favorite seasons.

Sunshine through scarlet maple trees, children romping in rustling piles of freshly raked leaves. That's fall.

Some October I'm going to visit someplace where it happens every year. That place will be nowhere I know in the Ozarks.

October's too confusing here. Just last week it was summer; flowers were blooming, lilac bushes thought it was spring, air conditioners were humming all over town.

Tuesday morning it was summer--sweltering, sticky, short-sleeve summer. We drove to work with the car windows rolled down. But, before lunch, it was winter. It came in on a north wind, followed by rain, ice, and snow flurries.

Friday night's football game was Buffalo's first annual Eskimo Bowl. The sub-zero wind chill blew wide spaces on the normally packed bleachers. Kids wrapped in blankets looked like displaced Sioux fleeing General Nelson Miles across the northern plains.

The weather watchers say we set a record Sunday

## River Of Used To Be

night. It dropped to ten degrees. At least the wind wasn't blowing. Friday's north wind felt a lot colder.

Single-digit chill factors are not common this time of year, even in these unpredictable Ozarks seasons. Most years we at least get a killing frost or two before the hard freeze.

Last week, winter blew blossoms off the marigolds.

Fall would have been more gentle. Fall would have clipped away at summer's grass and flowers a bit at a time. Winter just blew in like a reaper's scythe.

The weather may warm up this week, but it won't be fall. The leaves are off the trees. It's too late.

Winter may try to lull us with sunny days and warm Southern breezes, but ice in the dog dish doesn't lie.

Winter is another of my favorite seasons. I like the open woods and skeletal stands of naked trees. I like the bite of winter on my cheeks and the crunch of frozen earth beneath my feet. I like snow on hard, blue moonlit nights. I like winter.

But, I sure miss fall. Maybe winter will let her stop awhile next time through.

# Part Five

# TINSELTIME

## Christmas Columns

# Tinseltime

It must be Christmastime. There's tinsel stuck to my sock. Forget the twinkling lights. We can make them flicker anytime of year. Tinsel: That's the season's surest sign.

It's everywhere... everywhere it should be and everywhere it shouldn't be, lots of places other than gracefully complementing our Christmas tree.

Defying even the super vacuum for the garage and shop, silver strands lace the living room rug, braiding themselves into the piles, sparkling like crinkly wisps of Ozark streams seen from high on a late evening airplane flight.

Draped on the tree like the reflected twinkle from hoarfrost in airy flight, shimmering strands of silvery saran bring the amputated evergreen to life. Deceiving, slippery stuff, though, it just borrows its dancing light.

Tinsel. It's alive, you know.

Walk by the tree, then look at your calf or thigh. A few ambitious strands will have hitched a ride. Sterling as they may seem, they're nothing more than cheap holiday cockleburs, jumping on any leg that passes by.

Neither may these innocent angelic strands be trusted in the least. For all their glitter and pretense of purity, they're scoundrels when the lights go out.

Put out the lamps. Come morning you'll find on the rug a dozen brand new strands. Where the night before were only two or three, they'll have started a whole family.

Tinsel on my sock. Tinsel everywhere. Let a few strands loose here and there, and soon there's tinsel everywhere, multiplied like Ozarks rocks. Pick one up, two more take its place.

## Jim Hamilton

Don't think they're gone, either, when the tree is hauled away. Many will escape. Daffodils may bloom outside before the last strand is found. Some may even hide in corners of the house until the next holiday season comes around.

There are farms, I am told, where tinsel is grown, though I've never actually seen one. And I've never seen a University Extension Guide explaining the rearing of tinsel. But it must be something to see: Acres and acres of shimmering tinsel trees from tiny seedlings to towering foil giants.

There was a time, I am told, when tinsel farmers were a dying breed. There just wasn't much demand for the old heavy strands. Hybrid strains, they say, were the salvation of the tinsel farms. New, lighter cellophane varieties were cheaper to produce. Easy to seed and maintain, the new perennials made tinsel farming a brand new game.

Prolific little tinseli may grow to maturity in a season or two requiring hardly any care and scarcely any effort at all to process and package.

Now tinsel farmers have had their problems like others, problems from the EPA, DNR, FmHA, and USDA. All the pollution talk led many to forget their tinsel crops and put their lands in Conservation Reserve. There was a season or two, you might recall, when tinsel farmers suffered from drought. Strands of twelve and eighteen inches were mighty rare. Eight-inch nubbin strands wee about the longest that made their way to the holiday shelves.

Processors of tinsel have their troubles, too.

Consumers like their tinsel trimmed. City folks might imagine that tinsel grows in uniform twelve-inch strands, but farmers know that just isn't so.

Tinsel trimmings can't be burned, buried, or recycled like soda cans. On tinsel farms and processing plants across the country, there are growing piles of tinsel trash behind old sheds and barns.

But, no doubt, necessity will invent its own solution, and we need not fear for the future of tinsel farmers. As long as there are Christmas trees, the hardy few who raise and rear top quality tinseli will have a bright and shimmering future.

## Cedar Tree Tradition

A Christmas tree is a tradition of varying degrees.

For some folks, I suppose a crinkly old tinfoil tree will do, and some could care less if a dead tree or a plastic replica ever stood in the corner of their living room. For others, a trip to the local Christmas tree lot is a hallowed tradition.

But for us, no tinfoil, plastic, or imported tree will do. It has to be cedar, just like always.

The cedar Christmas tree tradition is a ritual of distinct stages: (1) Preparation, (2) Travel, (3) Cutting, and (4) Resurrection.

You can't simply decide to go cut a tree.

Preparation, or the warming-up-to-the-idea stage, generally starts before all the Thanksgiving leftovers are gone. Could be that it's inspired by the Macy's parade on television: That gets the youngsters to thinking.

Soon the nagging begins: "When are we gonna get a tree?" "What are we doing this weekend, Dad?" "All my friends have their trees up." "We'll probably never

## Jim Hamilton

get a tree. Mom doesn't want one anyway."

It takes about two weeks of prodding.

The day arrives. Two weeks of youngsters' pleadings have done its duty. Recovered from breakfast with Santa, the parade, and late-night television, I'm ready to head for the brush patch.

Now, that takes more preparation. First, I have to dig out my old oversized Air Force fatigue jacket and my leather gloves, neither of which are intimidated by dry cedar needles.

Then, we all have to put on boots, blue jeans, and all the rest of the raggedy outdoor gear we can find because the wind is raw and the ground squishy down where we look for trees.

An old bow saw and a double-bitted axe in hand, we pile into the truck and head south for Grandpa's farm.

Now there are lots of trees closer to home, and likely better ones, but we didn't have to ask to cut Grandpa's trees. We were expected.

The cutting is the most exciting part of the ritual, and the best exercise.

After warming by the woodstove, Angela, Melissa, and I head for the brush. Climbing across the barnyard fence, we turn our faces to the northwest wind and trek for the swampy north side of Dad's forty acres. Down on the branch is where the most cedars grow.

Weaving our way between bushy cedars, we search for the perfect one to kill and take into the house. "How about this one?" Angela yells as she lopes across a glade--splat, splat, squish--to a giant deserving of National Historic Site status.

Just kidding, I think.

## River Of Used To Be

"This is a good one," Meslissa says, turning like Vanna White to point out a shapely cedar.

A double: Two trees grown so close together they look like one. So it proceeds, tree after tree: Too tall, too full, lopsided, not green enough, too bare, too scrawny.

Finally, in the distance, we spy the perfect tree in the old hayfield fence row. Perfect, but grown a little crooked weaving its way around the wire.

Nobody will notice. We've spent nearly an hour and looked at nearly every tree on forty acres. They're all starting to look better.

The perfect tree wasn't. But we cut it down anyway because we didn't know how short it was 'til we cut it off above the crooked part.

Just up the fence row we found the really perfect tree. It was crooked too, but with counter-balancing bends to make it stand straight.

It was at least a quarter-mile from the house, too. A long drag. Very traditional. I could have driven the truck to the back of the hayfield, but I never planned to be there. We started out down on the branch and, back toward the house, tree in tow, we headed. One girl carried the axe, the other the saw, trading once. The steel saw handle was cold.

Resurrecting a felled cedar tree is an exasperating tradition. But in keeping with the spirit of the ritual, it cannot be accomplished too easily or too quickly.

It's dark now, of course. The rest must be done in the light of the seventy-five watt bulb on the windswept carport.

Once the tree is unloaded, the first step is to trim off some of the ragged lower branches and cut a smooth

## Jim Hamilton

base. After sawing at least a half-dozen poker chip-sized cedar slices off the trunk, it's even.

Mounting a fifty-pound tree in a flimsy three-legged stand is a tradition I could do without. But, we've never had anything better, and I don't know if anything better exists. If not, somebody ought to invent it.

The stamped metal legs bowed like the front end of an overloaded nag. It took a couple of one-bys and nails to shore it up, but finally the resurrected tree stood as if on its own.

Outside the house.

Keeping with tradition, we forced the tree through the kitchen door, showering the floor with little green holiday reminders, and carried it to its allocated area of the living room.

Too big. Too tall.

Funny how it looked a lot smaller in the fence row. Back outside it went. Soon the carport looked like a cedar's barber shop as I put my rusty hedge trimmers to work giving the hallowed tree a crew cut.

Almost perfect. Nothing tinsel won't cover. And so what if the stand is a little tilted? Just have to add water more often.

The kids love it.

Dee wonders why people bring dead trees in the house. But she still helps decorate it.

Tradition.

It doesn't have to make sense. It's Christmas.

River Of Used To Be

# Picture Of Despair

It was an image of despair.

A thin young man stood on the curb of a busy street holding a sign with an appeal to passing motorists: "Desperut. Will work for food."

It might have been a Walker Evans photo from the impoverished South of the 1930s; a compelling drama of despair compressed into a single black-and-white photograph.

But it wasn't. It was in full and living color--blue jeans, white shirt, bright Christmas decorations on nearby stores.

It was the last Saturday of November, 1990, in Springfield, Missouri, not nearly sixty years ago in Birmingham. It was not a photo, but a thin young man standing on a curb at the corner of Battlefield and Fremont as holiday shoppers zipped carelessly by.

I saw him across two lanes of traffic. Like others, I didn't stop. I thought about turning around. I couldn't give him work, but I could have given him a meal. I could have, but I didn't. I was afraid I was late to a meeting I had to make. Or maybe I was just afraid.

I'm a skeptic, used to a world in which anyone who is willing to work can find a job of sorts.

Then comes a compelling image, a hungry young man not pleading for charity, but for opportunity . . . for nothing more than a chance to earn his next meal.

His image haunts me as I hope it does thousands of others who passed him this past Saturday, for I fear he is not one, but one of many who will enjoy few blessings this holiday.

### Jim Hamilton

## A Christmas Gift

It was nearly one o'clock.

Roger, home from kindergarten just long enough to have finished his lunch of macaroni and cheese with hot dogs, stood on the living room couch, his knees curled in the back cushion.

Pulling the sheer curtain aside, he watched out the picture window for the mailman, just as he had nearly every day since October.

"Do you think we'll get something today from Johnny?" Roger shouted at his mother, who was still cleaning up the kitchen.

"Well, I certainly hope so," she responded. "That ol' couch can't take much more."

"Yeah. Maybe he'll send me a Christmas present like he did when he was in Germany."

"Don't get your hopes up," said Roger's mother, walking into the room. "They don't have stores there like they do in Germany."

A heavy expression settled across the boy's face as he turned back to watch for the mailman. "well, I know Johnny will get me something. He always does."

Roger heard the mailman's old Ford long before it pulled up to the mailbox. He watched as Vern stuffed a handful of letters and cards, several holiday catalogs, the local newspaper, and a small brown carton into the mailbox. "Mom! There's a package. I bet it's from Johnny," shouted Roger as he bounced from the couch and bounded out the door.

He came back in clutching an armful of holiday mail, dumped it all in his mother's lap as she waited on the couch, then climbed beside her on the worn cushions

## River Of Used To Be

as she proceeded to shuffle through the letters. Roger immediately grabbed the small brown box. It was heavy. "Open this one, Mom. Is it from Johnny? I'll bet he sent me some army bullets."

To Mom, Dad, and Roger, Route 1, the package read.

"It sure is. Let's see what he's done now."

Mom carefully peeled back the layers of brown paper until she got to a small plastic asprin bottle wrapped in a letter written on yellow note paper. She set the bottle aside and unfolded the note.

"What's he say? Why is he sending us asprin?"

Leaning back so Roger could look at the letter too, Mom began to read the note from her elder son:

*Dear Mom, Dad, and especially my little brother, Roger:*

*Merry Christmas from somewhere in the Saudi Arabian desert. As you might imagine, I haven't had much chance to go Christmas shopping. I don't even know where the closest Wal-Mart is.*

*I've been thinking about you all a lot, wishing I could be home, and wishing I could send you something. Sorry, Roger, the Ninja Turtle stuff I promised will have to wait 'til I get back.*

*You have to open the bottle to see what I have sent. Don't think I'm crazy from the heat. Pour it carefully into one of your crystal dishes, Mom, and put in on the mantle by our pictures. It's desert sand, but not common sand.*

*First of all, this sand came from under my boots. A lot of us have walked on this sand. But this bottleful is even more special. I funneled it through the palm of my*

## Jim Hamilton

*hand. Sift it through your hands as you pour it from the bottle, and it will be like I was there holding yours again, just like we used to as Dad asked the blessing over Christmas dinner.*

*This is sand from everywhere over here. I've watched it blow in clouds so thick you couldn't see the sun. No telling where this sand has been, or where it's bound. Imagine the stories it could tell.*

*Consider this holy sand. It was not far from here that creation began. It's possible that in these tablespoons of sand are a few grains of dirt from Eden; dust that once passed through God's hands in the creation of man.*

*Moved across deserts by Arabian winds, or carried on the soles of pilgrim's feet, some grains in the bottle I've sent may have once passed through Moses' fingers, or shifted beneath the feet of Israelites in the wilderness.*

*If these sands could talk, no doubt they'd tell of the prophets they had seen, of the rise and fall of Jericho, of the generations of Abraham.*

*Shifted by the winds, these are sands that Joseph and Mary, shepherds and wise men crossed in the first Christmas season. Imagine, even, that the reddish grains bear the blood of Jesus, or that of Christian knights slain in his name during the great Crusades.*

*I know it doesn't look like much, this little bottle of sand, and it's certainly nothing rare. Over here, it's everywhere. But, don't think of it as just gritty dirt; think of it as sand from the bleeding heart of a land ravaged since history began. Put it on the mantle beside my picture from boot camp and remember me, your soldier in the sand.*

Mom didn't finish the letter just then. She put it down, stood up and walked over to the china cabinet, took out a small crystal sugar bowl, and returned to the sofa. Setting the bowl on the coffee table, she took the asprin bottle and popped off the plastic cap.

"Roger, give me your hand," she said in a quietly broken voice. Roger soberly reached out his right hand. his mother took it in her left, held both over the crystal bowl, and gently poured a little bit of sand over their open palms.

She set the empty bottle down and carried the crystal bowl to the fireplace mantle, placing it by Johnny's picture.

Then, she did something that made no sense at all to Roger. Though it was the middle of the day, and there was no need for extra light, between the sand and the picture of her firstborn, she lit a candle.

## Holiday Season Like Vacation

The Christmas season arrives like a long-delayed vacation. We await it with anticipation, welcome it with grand expectations.

Like second-string quarterbacks suddenly hearing our names called by the coach--"Get your butt off the bench and get in there"--we charge onto the holiday gridiron with bloodletting lust.

Undaunted, we challenge crowded malls, parties, parades, programs, and dozens more Christmas frolics finally, but happily, falling on our flustered faces in the holiday mire, exhausted.

Fun: We work at it harder than work. Just like vacation.

Christmas Day, then, is like the last day of a six-state trip; the long, last leg of grueling fun. Home is just around the next bend on Scenic Route 25.

All humbuggery aside, I confess to childish eagerness on Christmas Day. No doubt about who will be the first kid up on Christmas morning. Me.

I guess it's just a habit I got into as a youngster, and the old biological clock has me programmed for life.

Every December 25th, I awaken at 3:00 a.m. And again at 4:00, and then at 5:00, never later than 6:00.

It's no longer the anticipation of gifts that excites me, though. It's the excitement of discovering what has been left under the tree by Mrs. Claus.

## The Truth About Santa

Is there really a Santa Claus?

The question is asked every Christmas; we've all heard it. We've even asked once or twice.

Common sense provides the answer: No.

The whole notion is preposterous. The idea of a fat little man who slides down chimneys and doesn't even get soot in his flowing white beard, who brings bags of toys to all good children, who flies through the December skies from his home at the North Pole in a magic sleigh pulled by midget reindeer one of which has a glowing red nose . . . . The whole scenario is quite unbelieveable.

Is there really a Santa Claus? Of course not. The whole thing is a fairy tale created to make children behave--a nasty trick the less gullible like to play on their kids.

But, then again, if there is no Santa Claus, why do

## River Of Used To Be

most of us remember him?

Maybe you never actually saw him, but don't you remember him? Think about it.

Remember a Christmastime long ago when you stood in a long line at the department store, tugging at Mom's hand to get a peek at the man in the red flannel suit at the front of the line? You finally crawled upon his lap and told him your Christmas wishes, confident they, or at least most of them, would be granted. You noticed as you squirmed on his lap, that he wasn't as fat as Santa should be. But, you knew he wasn't really Santa, just one of his helpers. He had to have lots of helpers. You were young, but you were no dummy. After all, Santa had a lot to do around Christmastime. There were lots of lists to read. He needed helpers. You understood, and you dreamed of the real Santa visiting you on Christmas Eve.

And remember Christmas Eve? You left a glass of milk and some of Mom's chocolate fudge on the coffee table along with a note to Santa. You hung a stocking on the fireplace, if you had one. If you had no fireplace, you just put it up where Santa was sure to find it--maybe at the foot of your bed.

Santa, after all, didn't always slide down the chimney. That much you knew was just a story. He came in the front door with his bag of toys.

Then came Chrismas morning! Before the sun was up you peeked around the corner to see the pile of toys and bright packages sparkling under the Christmas tree, and you called to Mom and Dad, "Can we get up now?"

You found the stocking stuffed with all sorts of goodies--candy, fruit, nuts, little toys.

## Jim Hamilton

Remember those Christmas mornings? You knew Santa had come. It was not a game, nor a fairy tale.

Mom and Dad could never have afforded to buy all those toys and clothes and Christmas candies, times being what they were.

Besides that, the milk and fudge were gone.

No Santa Claus? Well, there certainly was one back then, if you'll remember carefully.

And there is today if you're looking for him. I've seen him. He's in the sparkle of a little girl's eyes, in the gleam of her smile, and the anxious giggle when she talks about him and the toys he's going to bring her.

That's proof enough for me.

But there's more. There's hundreds of letters from kids who sent their Christmas wishes to old St. Nick.

"I love you, Santa," many of them say. I would hate to think all that love is being thrown away.

If there's no Santa Claus, then a four year-old girl has no Christmas dreams. There's no Christmas magic, no Christmas love in children's hearts.

## Santa Drops In On Cinder Creek

McCormick Stillings was down at the courthouse the other day as we went in to pay taxes.

Mac had made himself at home on the east steps, a crowd of youngsters was gathered all around him, and he started to tell them the story about how Santa Claus dropped into Cinder Creek one night and nearly didn't make on the rest of his rounds.

It happened on Christmas Eve, 1940. Ol'

# River Of Used To Be

McCormick was just a kid, about twelve as he recalled. His brother, Evan, the one we lost in Korea, was ten that year.

Mac and Evan were walking home after a Christmas party at the Methodist Church over on the north end of town. They took the road that crossed the steel bridge over Cinder Creek. The Stillings place was down a lane just past the fork to Buzzard Crest, not more than a quarter of a mile past the bridge.

It was an overcast night, just barely freezing with a promise of snow in the air.

The boys walked the familiar road, talking about the Christmas party, things they hoped to see under the tree next morning, and sucking on peppermint candy canes from a bag of goodies they got at the church.

Mac carried the kerosene lantern. Traveler, the boy's bluetick hound, padded out just ahead of them, sometimes just scarcely visible in the outer reaches of the lantern's yellow glow.

As they talked and ambled toward home, Evan searched the heavy sky looking, even through the clouds, for the Christmas Star they'd learned about in Sunday School.

Suddenly Evan stopped and grabbed his brother by the coat cuff. "Mac! There it is. I saw it. The star the Wise Men saw. Just over our house. Look, Mac!"

Mac stopped, set the lantern down behind them, and looked into the dark east. Not even a house light could be seen on the far ridges. "There," Evan pointed, with a half-chewed candy cane in his sticky fist. "You can just barely see it."

Then, Mac saw it too. A faint glimmer in the sky like the shine off a tin can lid dropped into a cistern. It

## Jim Hamilton

was coming closer.

Standing in the middle of the road, the boys watched the light nearing, getting brighter every second. Traveler came back to see why they'd stopped. Without dropping his eyes from the sky, Evan lowered his right hand to pet the old hound, hardly noticing as Traveler licked his sweet, sticky fingers.

Mac and Evan stood there transfixed by the light. "Maybe it's a falling star," Mac started to say, but got out only a gasp when he saw, not one light, but dozens, in all colors. Then they heard such a crash, jingling and rattling, like dropping a dozen silverware drawers on a hard kitchen floor.

Then it was dark, and not a sound was heard but the wind swirling around the old bridge.

In a moment, they heard a soft, scuffling sound, and a tinkling or two like a shopkeeper's bell. The boys looked at one another without a word. Mac grabbed the lantern and they walked cautiously toward the sounds. As they neared the bridge Traveler bayed, then slunk back to the boys, growling lowly through bared teeth.

Holding the lantern high, the boys walked toward the bridge. "Ow!" Evan blurted as he tripped over something and fell to the ground. He looked down and saw a broken jack-in-the-box.

A crunching sound was next as Mac stepped on a toy truck.

Evan put his foot down on a rubber duck that made a squeaking sound.

Suddenly, they heard the clop, clop, clop of hoofbeats racing across the floor of the wooden bridge.

At the far end sat a fat little man in a furry red suit, the spitting image of old St. Nick, right down to the

## River Of Used To Be

bloom in his cheeks.

"Reckon this here's a dream, or one of those hallucinations," said Mac. "Pinch me on the ear. See if it hurts."

"Well, well," the fat man chuckled as he saw the boys approach. "Come closer with that lantern, boys. No real harm done here that I can see, but I'd be obliged for the use of that light."

The boys came closer, and what they saw left little doubt in their skeptical eyes. If there was ever a Santa Claus, this was the guy.

Toys were strewn all about, harness leather lay all in a pile, a sled with a crumpled runner lay on its side at the east end of the bridge, and an entire herd of reindeer huddled behind the fat little man just at the edge of the light.

What had occurred became quickly apparent, even to those youngsters of twelve and ten. Ol' St. Nick had crashed his sleigh into the Cinder Creek bridge.

The boys sat down on some sturdy snare drums, growing more at ease all the while, as the fat little man stoked his cherry-wood pipe, called his reindeer in close, and stroked groaning Traveler behind the ear.

As the boys resumed sucking their peppermint canes, Santa explained the source of his misfortune. It was all the fault, he surmised, of some naughty Polk County boys earlier in the night. Those boys--he knew their names--must have put loco weed in those reindeer treats. Why, his dependable eight could hardly fly straight, couldn't help but fly into that bridge that night.

But, he reckoned they could straighten up and fly right by now, so enlisted the boys to help him on his way.

## Jim Hamilton

While Evan held the lantern, Mac helped the fat little man gather up all his spilled merchandise. Both boys watched as the little man ran his hand over the bent runner, one end to the other. Magically, it was good as new.

The reindeer, most friendly by now, let the boys slip them in harness while the fat man loaded his sleigh.

When all was repaired and ready to go, the little man climbed aboard his sleigh. "Just one more thing I have to ask, boys. I surely appreciate all your help, but I'd still be obliged for the use of your light for the rest of the night. I can fix a sled, but can't do much with a battery that's dead."

What could they say? "Well, reckon we could," Mac replied. "We can find our way to the house all right. Had to lots of times," he assured the fat little man, and handed him the lantern.

With that the sled began to slide with a bit of a screech and the reindeer hooves clopped once or twice. Then, the boys saw their lantern light lift into the sky and disappear into the night.

They looked at one another. "Reckon it was a dream. Pinch me to see. Now, Evan, where'd you lose that light?"

The next morning they awoke well before daylight, crawled from the bed, and went to see what had been left under the tree.

There, in the flicker of the faint firelight, sat their old lantern, and beside it, two new ones, a couple of Barlow knives, a Western Flyer sled, and two shiny Schwinn bikes.

And, hanging from the tree, was a new leather collar with a gleaming brass plate. "Traveler" was all it read, but as Mac recalled, that old dog wore it until the day he died.

It was several years before either of the boys said much about that Christmas Eve. After all, they reckoned it was just a dream. But, many a time as we walked across the bridge, Mac or Evan would point out a twisted steel beam on the bridge's east end and say, "See what a dent a sleigh can make?"

Now Mac tells the tale to any who will listen, and tells it like it's so.

Nobody here is about to tell him it isn't.

## Elmo, The Stable Elf

Just when you thought you had heard every Santa story ever told, along comes another. This one is a tale about Elmo.

Elmo, the son of Durward the Elder and Madame Anastasia of the Confectionery, was always ill-suited to the traditional trades of the elfin race.

As a young elfling, his schoolmates and teachers called him "Elmo the Awkward," not because he often tripped, but because wherever he was, he never fit.

In elf gym class, for example, he rolled a basketball to bowl down the cheerleaders rather than toss it through the hoop.

As an apprentice in Santa's toy wagon shop, he preferred sprinkling fairy dust on wheels rather than putting them on the axles. Either will work at home, but once away from the North Pole, fairy-dusted wheels won't roll.

Santa tried him in other jobs, but he didn't fit. He

## Jim Hamilton

was chased by his Uncle Lionel from the toy train shop for reversing the locomotive's polarity, and he was literally tossed from the candy cane kitchen for licking stripes off the peppermint sticks.

The last job he held in the Christmas shops was working at the foot of his patient mother's skirts. But, alas, Elmo found pecan divnity much too divine, and was hustled from the confectionery kitchen with marshmallowy goo still white on his lips.

By the time he was a scant 142 years old, his service as one of Santa's elves was doomed. Not one job remained for the undisciplined elf, and he might have been relegated to some governmental cabinet job but for the intervention of Santa himself.

Yes, it was the old man and not a common elf who gave Elmo one last chance, a decision which would prove providential, to say the least.

Elmo was made a stable elf, a chore he could do all by himself. There was nothing to build. All Elmo had to do was feed Santa's tiny reindeer, keep the stable clean, and have the sleigh polished for Christmas Eve.

Now, flying reindeer have a special diet of pumpkin seeds and popcorn balls with plenty of root beer to drink twice a day, every day. Keeping them properly fed was a most important job, especially near Christmas Eve. Short a reindeer his root beer and he can barely jump, let alone fly from the North Pole to the south and back again.

A more prideful elf might have felt demeaned by stable work, but Elmo understood the importance of his chores and set about them diligently. There was never a stray pumpkin seed or popcorn kernel to crunch under Santa's boot.

## River Of Used To Be

Besides, this job as stable elf gave Elmo more opportunity than ever to visit with Santa Claus. Old St. Nick came to the stable at least twice a day. He admired the sheen Elmo's care and brushing put on the animal's coats, and never missed telling a bedtime story to Donner, Blitzen, and all the rest.

Madame Anastasia was very proud of her little boy, and Santa bragged often of his exceptional stable elf. So, one afternoon all the toyshop elves agreed, and the confectionery and candy cookers brought him a special treat--a big basket of chocolate peanut clusters and malted milk balls.

Elmo was very pleased they had forgotten about fairy-dusted wagon wheels and backward-running trains. He thanked them graciously and said not a word about the flour they tracked in on his floor.

That night, after feeding Santa's reindeer their usual fare, Elmo called them around and offered to share his candy reward, for they, after all, had behaved mighty well these past months too.

That was the night they all learned about the nose. For the older eight, the peanut clusters and the malted milk balls were just a tasty dessert. But for Rudolph, called until then just "Ol' Number Nine," the chocolate candies held quite a surprise.

First it was a blush, but with another chocolate bite the blush began to grow. Before the basket was even half-empty, Rudolph's nose had attained its now-famous rosy glow.

Elmo was aghast, afraid he had done something wrong or that Rudolph was ill. He put down his chocolate in the middle of a bite and was about to summon Santa to see for himself when the stable door

## Jim Hamilton

flung open wide.

There in the door stood St. Nick, buckets in either hand, leading an entire elfin bucket brigade. "Why, I thought the stable was on fire," he said, still not sure it wasn't.

Then he moved closer to look at Number Nine. He had seen such a thing on radio towers and airplane noses, but never on an airborne reindeer's snout.

He asked Elmo what it was all about, then helped try to figure it out. Rudolph's health, it seemed, was none the worse, but the candy went back to the kitchen nonetheless. Elmo didn't get much sleep, partly because it was nearly daylight before that nose ceased to glow. The next morning when Santa came down, he and Elmo discussed the phenomenon of the previous night, and determined that some Christmas Eve he might have use for that unusual light.

Well, you know the rest. Ol' Gene Autry told it pretty well in his song, but he never told you about Elmo.

See, ever since that night portrayed in that song, Elmo has had a special job on foggy Christmas Eves. While Santa is packing up his sleigh, Elmo feeds chocolate peanut clusters and malted milk balls to Rudolph, hitched up in the lead. By the time Santa's ready to go, that nose is all aglow and so is Elmo, who always goes along in case the glow should dim to just a glimmer. Santa has a lot to do delivering toys and stuffing stockings; there's hardly time for stoking Rudolph's coals.

That's Elmo's other job. While Santa works beneath your tree, Elmo sniffs your chocolate out. He never takes much, just a piece or two... that carmel that nobody ate, the toffee crunch that mysteriously disappeared from the candy dish. At every stop on Santa's route, Elmo grabs a peanut cluster here, a cherry cordial there--just enough for Rudolph's nose.

And, if there's a piece or two for Elmo left over, who knows? It isn't *his* nose that glows.

## Celebration Of Christmas Promise

This is our first Christmas season without Angela, the first year in twenty she has no gifts beneath a Christmas tree.

This season there is no holiday gaiety, no twinkling lights, no Santa Claus in our house. There is no Christmas tree, no children's stockings to be filled.

There is no festivity in this season, but there is celebration; in our hearts a quiet, solemn celebration of the birth of Jesus 2,000 years ago in Bethlehem.

As that first Christmas fulfilled the prophecies and promises of Scripture, we are assured in this season, 1991, that the promises that followed that birth will also be fulfilled. Angela is celebrating her first Christmas with the Child of Bethlehem. She is joined with family-- her uncle Stephen, her great-grandmother Daly, and others she is just getting to know.

It must be quite a reunion. Yet, maybe selfishly, I wish she were here this Christmas. The pain of her absence is slow to subside. Angela is on our minds constantly, in our hearts with every beat.

The only thing we want for Christmas, Santa can't bring.

But, Santa is not much in our thoughts this

## Jim Hamilton

Christmas. The only gift worth cherishing was given 2,000 years ago with Jesus' birth. Jesus promised life eternal to anyone who trusted in him. Angela took him at his word. In that, we quietly celebrate.

It is not a merry Christmas. These holidays are not happy. Angela would have been twenty on New Year's Eve. Yet, in this most bleak and dismal of seasons, the Christmas Star shines more brightly that ever.

My only Christmas wish is, no matter how joyous or how somber your season that you, too, might quietly celebrate the Christmas Star's unfading light.

# Part Six

# HAMBONE RIDGE

## Quiet Voices In The Wind

## A Place To Slip Away

About halfway between Buzzard Crest and nowhere in particular, just this side of anyplace certain, and not far from Cinder Creek, Hambone Ridge rises in the Ozarks timber.

Folks who know it say you can't get there from here. Fact is, you can if you can take directions.

The denizens of Buzzard Crest and Cinder Creek alike are known to climb the ridge from time to time. Buzzards and Carpwaters both sometimes find a rise and listen to quiet voices in the wind.

Hambone Ridge. A place to slip away, lean against a white oak tree, and look out across where you've been. It's not on any map, though it's not so hard to find. It's not so much a place as it is a point of view.

## Halloween

Summertime, this ridge is an amicable retreat, a hospitable place.

The mosses, ferns, moist leaves, and unnamed flowers peeking from crevices in the shelf rock emit a musky perfume. The breeze rises softly up the south slope and whispers in the trees. It's a tranquil place, unremittingly safe.

But those cradle days are past. The hard nights of October at last awaken spirits from the windswept leaves, rattle ancient bones in the skeletons of moonlit trees.

Spectres unnamed, unseen, though their footsteps heard and their damp breath sensed on the nape of the neck walk the barren ridge every Halloween.

Neither man nor animal dares climb the ridge

# Jim Hamilton

that one night, warned away by the few who have tried and the night survived.

Indian ghosts, Sauk and Fox we're told, fought this night and died. Now, though their bones have long returned to Earth, the warriors' spirits stalk the ridge where once they fought, forever to fight that forbidden duel on Halloween night.

Doubter, you have but to climb the ridge this Halloween, sit and wait against the gnarled trunk of the ancient post oak Indian tree. Press your palms into the earth, close them tight and grasp, feel the warmth of the warriors' blood.

Press your head against the bark and feel the bristles rise. Lift your eyes toward the point, watch the hatchets rise and fall in the moonlit dancing of the trees. Hear the scuffling moccasins of warriors locked in their eternal death struggle just beyond the dim moonlight behind the forked tree. Hear the shuffling of the leaves.

From past Anvil Point and just over the precipice, a Sauk death song rises on the lifting wind, the low chant of a fallen warrior entreating ancient spirits to claim his soul, though on this evil night they surely won't.

The wind subsides, the death song dies, the leaves are quiet. You press in the cold moonlit night more closely to the ancient tree.

Drop . . . drip. Droplets fall from a snaggled limb, warm upon the back of your hand.

The warrior's blood that stains the tree against which you sit stains your hand with its guilt.

In the midnight moon you'll beat an ancient path from this unhallowed place and never doubt against the tales of Hambone Ridge.

# River Of Used To Be

## Cloyd And Brody On Anvil Point

Anvil Point juts out of the end of this ridge as hard and bare as its name suggests.

Where the ridge slopes off to Cinder Creek, the point affords a considerable view of the bottom clear down to the Niangua, and at night you can see the lights of Buzzard Crest.

Folks have beaten a trail to that point for as long as their trails have crossed this country. Of late, the most frequent visitors have been Cloyd Carpwater and Brody Buzzard, though seldom at the same time.

But, on Saturday afternoon the same notion struck these two old adversaries, and both set out for a few quiet hours up on Anvil Point.

Cloyd was already there when Brody came shuffling down the trail. He was propped against a blackjack, just stoking up his pipe. Brody, a chaw of Redman in his jaw, managed a civil "Howdy" which was returned, then he walked a few steps past Cloyd, closer to the edge of the point. For ten minutes or so he just stood there, hands in the back pockets of his overalls, surveying the familiar bottoms. After a while he ambled back to Cloyd who was, by then, leaned back in a cloud of armoatic smoke.

There followed some words about a baseball game between the Cinder Creek Cyclones and the Buzzard Crest Batburners, the last game the two teams ever played on a dusty diamond at the foot of Hambone Ridge just days before the war broke up the teams in 1941.

It was a long time ago, they reckoned.

The two men sat quiet for a spell. Cloyd tapped

the ashes out of his pipe onto a blackened rock, evidence he had been there before. Brody dug into his back pocket for his Redman.

"Reckon they'll ever get that dam?" Brody asked, spitting on the rocks to punctuate his question.

"Will if they want it," Cloyd said, taking his pipe from his mouth. "Ever know folks down in Queen City not to get their way?"

"Reckon they got to have the water, but it don't seem like it oughter be ours they've got to have."

"Oughten be," said Cloyd, clenching his pipe in his teeth. "Seems ought-tos don't count for much these days."

Brody shuffled, stuffed his tobacco back into his pocket, and spit at a gray lizard sunning on a log. The lizard scurried to the far side.

Cloyd was stoking up a fresh pipeful of tobacco. "Cain't imagine a town needin' so much water. S'pose they'll just flush most of it down their toilets. Just plain waste it."

"Yeah, s'pose."

Brody walked back to the edge. "They'll take the town and move it to high ground, they say."

"Cain't move a town," said Cloyd. "Just move people and houses. Don't move towns. Like this here blackjack, a town dies where it grows. Can cut it down and move it, but then it ain't a tree, just what could be cut from one. Town's the same. you can cut it up and move it and give it the same name, but it ain't the same. Cain't be."

"Shoot, Cloyd, you been suckin' on that pipe too long. Startin' to ramble like ol' W.W. does in *The Bugle*." Brody responded, pulling a wad from his gums.

## River Of Used To Be

"No sense in us worryin' about it," the old Buzzard continued. "There's lots of other places they got to look at before they get clear up here. Besides, we'll be dead and buried before they figure out what they ought to do."

"Maybe," said Cloyd, tapping the ashes from his pipe. "But I always took pains not to go noodlin' in my Sunday best. Don't figure to start in the hereafter."

"Well then, Cloyd, maybe you oughta leave that Sunday suit hanging in the closet. Wouldn't be the first fella to greet St. Peter in his long handles."

"S'pose not," Cloyd mumbled, rising from his spot against the oak. "I'll study on it."

Brody turned to look out over the bottoms. Cloyd ambled on up the trail and soon the shuffle of his steps was lost in the rustle of the wind in the trees.

Brody stood on the point a while longer, just looking out over the bottoms. It was a fair walk back to Buzzard Crest on the other side. Though he saw smoke from his house. Bunea must be baking.

The ridges were turning calico; sumac and sassafrass along the edges of the fields were already afire, like the creeping vines on naked walnut trees. Spitting once more at the lizard, he turned and walked up the trail, disappearing, like Cloyd, into the woods.

Out on the point, the gray lizard moved cautiously back to the top of the tobacco-splattered log, avoiding the wet, brown patches, settling on the precipitous tip of Anvil Point, soaking up the last warming rays of the late September sun.

# Jim Hamilton

## Bucket Seat

It appears Cloyd Carpwater has staked a permanent claim on his studying spot on Anvil Point, under the blackjack oak where he always does most of his most serious contemplations.

Cloyd came trudging across the ridge the other evening lugging an old car seat on his back, a shiny, vinyl bucket seat, blood-red as sumac leaves in September.

With a gut-felt grunt and a gust of stale tobacco wind from deep in his chest, he like to fell over as he heaved the thing against the tree.

Catching his breath, he pulled some bailing wire from his back pocket and unfolded it. Reckoning on the length, he snipped off a couple feet or so with the long-nosed pliers he kept in the side pocket of his overalls.

Scooting the seat snugly against the tree trunk, he ran the wire through the metal seat frame and around the tree, then twisted the two wires together with his pliers, snipping off the ends of the knot with the precision of a surgeon.

With the seat secure, he gave her a try, scrunching it around in the gravel like a cowboy settling in on the back of a bull in the Number 3 chute at the National Finals Rodeo.

No good. He would be throwed for sure. He unfolded out of the Mustang saddle and kicked around in the leaves until he found a flat rock just the right size. Carrying it over to the chair, he wedged the platter-sized rock under the seat frame and gave it a couple of sturdy kicks.

He again lowered himself into the red bucket, steadying himself with a hand on the rough bark of the blackjack. Better than the armchair on the front porch. And a lot better situated.

Cloyd pushed his cap back off his forehead and leaned back in the blood-red vinyl. a light wind brought leaves prattling to the ground all around him. Leaves fluttered off the end of Anvil Point and drifted like lazy swallow toward the bottom.

Cloyd pulled his pipe and a tin of Prince Albert from the bib pocket of his overalls. This was one job he was pleased to be done with. Been intending to get him a chair up here for the last two years.

He then fired up his pipe and settled back to study on his next big chore: Listening to the seasons change on the ridge.

## Last Day Of Coffeepot Rock

When Ezra was fourteen he noodled a thirty-pound catfish from under Coffeepot Rock.

Noodling was a nervy undertaking, even for the old-time rivermen--plunging into the roiling blue-green depths of Cinder Creek to poke about in a root-tangled catfish lair. For Ezra, it had been a necessary initiation into a fraternity as sacred and mysterious as the weathered faces of the uncles, cousins, and neighbors who welcomed him into their brotherhood.

The memories of those days flowed as crisp and deep as the creek which had harbored those giant cats as Ezra sat on the ledge of Coffeepot Rock this fair fall morning some sixty years since.

A light breeze carried russet, red, and yellow leaves rattling lightly to the rippling surface of the

## Jim Hamilton

stream. At the end of the day they lay like one of Sarah's old quilts piled against a fallen sycamore top.

Another season's blackened leaves covered much of the gravel stream bottom below the rock where Ezra watched a small carp rooting a muddying trail along the shoal of the once blue noodlin' hole. Had he taken a notion, Ezra could have waded across without getting his pockets wet.

A gust of wind scoured dust and scooted leaves from the sandy top of Coffeepot Rock as Ezra stood and reached into the hip pocket of his overalls for a pack of Redman.

Pulling a wad of tobacco from his cheek, he flipped it into the stream where it drifted to the bottom, disintegrating as it fell.

He pulled a fresh chew from his pouch and stuffed it into his mouth. Wiping his sticky fingers on faded overalls, he ambled back to his seat on the ledge.

In the brush across the stream, scratching in the leaves under a stand of paw paw trees, Ezra saw a dozen wild turkeys. As he sat quietly on the rock, two hens came close to the water's edge, stepping out of the shade and into the rising sunlight of mid-morning.

The quiet rustle of leaves was broken by a ring of voices across the bottom, and then the bellowing of bulldozers starting to work on the ridge. The turkeys disappeared into the shadows and horseweeds across the creek.

Ezra could see and smell black diesel smoke before he could see the yellow machines through the trees. The rising and falling rumble of engines and clattering track drew closer as Ezra remained nailed to his ledge.

## River Of Used To Be

Before he had worn out another chew, he heard the labor of engines and the crack of timber falling. Upstream, a hole opened with a crashing of trees in the arbor which guarded the creek. A yellow Cat of another breed moved into the stream.

The old noodler sat motionless on the rock, watching as the clear water turned brown.

When he could no longer see the bottom of the stream, he stood, pulled the wad of tobacco from his cheek, and tossed it into the chocolate milk-colored water.

Then, Ezra walked to where an ancient crevice divided the top of Coffeepot Rock. From his back pocket he pulled two old and oily sticks of dynamite saved from blasting stumps from the bottom years ago. Holding onto the long twisted fuses, he lowered the sticks until they wedged tight, then laid the long fuses across the top of the rock.

Pulling a kitchen match from his shirt pocket, he lit the fuses, and then turned and disappeared like the wild turkeys into the shadows under the paw paw trees.

From their house below the top of the hill, Sarah watched the old man step out of the brush on his return from the creek as she had most mornings of late. Sitting on the porch, she could see more clearly than he the milling of many yellow earth-moving machines and the new highway taking shape across the bottom. Farther across the ridges she could see the towering new hotels of West Cinder Creek and the spindly legs of a new roller coaster ride.

The dozers were clearing the way for a new bridge across Cinder Creek, not more than a hundred yards from the old ford built by the special road district

## Jim Hamilton

in '42.

The old road couldn't handle the tourist traffic, and city folks had no sense at all when it came to crossing at the ford. Ezra had pulled more than one fancy van from the creek.

The new road, the city folks' road, would cut right across the noodlin' hole.

There was talk of saving Coffeepot Rock, of the state buying much of Ezra's old place, maybe making a park or campground beside the new bridge. Folks in town were sure it would be used a lot.

Over the drone of the bulldozers, no one but Ezra heard the muffled blast and splash as Coffeepot Rock crumbled with the old man's past.

# Acknowledegements

　　I wrote the columns in *River Of Used To Be* unassisted. However, putting them into a book took a little help. It never would have happened without the support of the following:

* My wife, Dee, and my daughter, Melissa, who spent many hours alone while I worked on the book;
* Angela, my greatest fan, the memory of whom continues to inspire;
* Steve Schibler, whose assistance in taking the newspaper columns from newsprint to computer was invaluable;
* Jim Sterling, owner of the *Buffalo Reflex*, whose newspapers have provided me opportunity for creative expression, and whose personal encouragement has been unwavering;
* My newspaper staff, who have endured the writer, as well as the editor, and pitched in to get the paper out when all I could concentrate on was this book;
* The folks who have read my newspaper columns and told me they liked them. Without their support, I would have quit;
* The people of Dallas County, Missouri, whose images are reflected in the eddies of *River Of Used To Be*.